# American History
# CHALLENGE!

## A CLASSROOM QUIZ GAME

**THIRD EDITION**

MW00453662

**WALCH PUBLISHING**

E. Richard and
Linda R. Churchill

The classroom teacher may reproduce materials in this book for classroom use only.
The reproduction of any part for an entire school or school system is strictly prohibited.
No part of this publication may be transmitted, stored, or recorded in any form
without written permission from the publisher.

1     2     3     4     5     6     7     8     9     10

ISBN 0-8251-4358-6

Copyright © 1978, 1988, 1997, 2002
J. Weston Walch, Publisher
P.O. Box 658 • Portland, Maine 04104-0658
walch.com

Printed in the United States of America

# Contents

# To the Teacher

*American History Challenge!* generates real enthusiasm as it addresses the fundamentals of U.S. history. It is designed to be used for several purposes: as a fun and easy way to reinforce what is being studied, as a study guide, and as a review of the unit or a culminating activity. It challenges your students to remember important facts and encourages them to enjoy themselves in the process.

The format of *American History Challenge!* is similar to that of a popular television game show. A student is given the answer and is asked to provide the question. Questions are divided into categories, and the fact given as a question is actually stated ("First man to sign the Declaration of Independence"), not asked. Then the student response is given as a question ("Who is John Hancock?"). Many students will already be familiar with the format.

## How to Use This Book

Each topic, or game, consists of four general categories. Each question in each category has a point value. The easiest questions are worth 5 points, more difficult questions are worth 10 points, and the most difficult questions are worth 15 and 20 points. Categories do not always include the same number of questions in each game, nor are the values of the questions always exactly divided among 5, 10, 15, and 20 points.

Before you play the game with your students, it may prove effective to allow them to find the answers to, or study, the questions first. You may wish to reproduce the questions for a series of assignments, and then use a game as an evaluation, a further review, or a culmination of the unit. You may find that using the questions without a game is adequate. For these reasons, the answers are presented separately at the back of the book rather than with the questions.

Here are the directions for a typical game:

- Put the categories for the game to be played on the board with the point-value range.

- Divide the class into teams. Play begins when one student asks for a question from a given category with a given point value. For instance,

the student might say, "I want a 10-point question from the 'Those Who Dared' category."

- The game leader then reads a 10-point question from the requested category.

- Any student on the team may answer. The first person on the team to raise his or her hand is called on. (It may be the student who asked for the category to begin with.)

- If the answer is correct, record points for the team. The student who answered chooses the category and point value for the next question.

- If the answer is wrong, subtract the point value of the question from the team score. A student from the other team now has the chance to answer the question. Whoever answers the question correctly chooses the category and point value for the next question.

- If no one can answer the question, give the correct answer to the group. The student who last successfully answered a question chooses the next category and point value.

- When all the questions of a given point value have been used within a category, erase that point value. Continue with the other questions until the category is completely used.

- When all the questions in a category have been used, erase that category from the board. Continue until all the categories are erased and the game is over.

Feel free to modify *American History Challenge!* If you have stressed something in your class that is not included in this game, it is easy to add questions. Your students will quickly learn how to make questions for you in order to extend the game. Your class can play the same game more than once, which will help them remember material more easily.

No matter how you use *American History Challenge!* it is an entertaining and stimulating way to review, and it's an excellent change-of-pace activity. You'll find your students eager to play over and over again.

# AMERICAN HISTORY CHALLENGE!

## Questions

# Concepts in History

**1**

| HISTORY MAKERS | HISTORICAL LOCATIONS | HISTORICAL TIMES | IDEAS IMPORTANT TO HISTORY |
|---|---|---|---|

**5**

**HISTORY MAKERS**

1. People who study about people, places, and events of the past

2. Person who actually sees some act or happening

3. Things that happen or occur

4. Scientist who studies ancient ruins and artifacts to learn about the past

**HISTORICAL LOCATIONS**

1. Land just beyond the settled edge of a nation

2. Settlements people made in lands away from their own nations

3. Large settled area conquered and controlled by a single power

4. North America, Central America, and South America in the 1400s

**HISTORICAL TIMES**

1. Way to measure the passage of days, months, and years

2. Time before history was written

3. Period of 100 years

4. Event used in the Christian calendar to measure time

5. Period of 10 years

6. Period after the Bronze Age when humans used tools made from iron

7. What A.D. stands for

8. An event or time that marks the beginning of a new development

**IDEAS IMPORTANT TO HISTORY**

1. Agreement between nations

2. Humans' belief in God or the supernatural

3. A group of people who make and carry out the laws by which people live

4. Agreement that ends a war

5. Group of people who make laws that others must obey

6. Attack in which hostile troops of one nation enter another nation

7. Term for the problem facing a nation with more people than it can support

8. Conflicts in which two parts of the same nation fight each other

**10**

©1978, 1988, 1997, 2002 Walch Publishing

9. Facts that point toward what is true and what is false about an event

10. Careful hunting for facts or truth

11. Idea about how something happened

12. Exact words of someone

13. Culture or ways of living of a society

---

14. The way people use resources to make and sell goods and services

15. Family of rulers

16. Empire-building by nations

17. A human-made object, such as a tool or weapon

---

9. Period of time figured from some particular date

10. Period of 20 years

11. Prehistoric period during which humans used tools made from stone

12. Period of 1,000 years

---

13. Long period of time

14. Period of approximately 33 years

---

5. Places where the first known civilizations were established

6. Term meaning any natural feature of the earth's surface

---

5. Friendly nation that helps another nation in a war

6. Scientific name for humans

---

7. Uncivilized people

8. Thoughts, beliefs, and methods of doing things that are handed down from ancestors

---

15

20

NOTES

# Geographic Concepts

**2**

## General Geographic Terms

1. A book of maps
2. A model of the earth
3. Half of a globe or sphere
4. Zero line of latitude
5. Weather conditions of an area over a period of years
6. The study and description of the earth
7. Any form of natural moisture falling from the sky
8. A geographical dictionary
9. An imaginary line equally distant from the North and South Poles
10. Mud composed of fine bits of rock and soil

## Landform Terms

1. Shapes of the earth's surface
2. One of the earth's seven major landmasses
3. Regions of flat or gently rolling land
4. An area of land surrounded by water on three sides
5. A mountain formed when melted rock is forced through the earth's surface
6. Land surrounded on all sides by water
7. A group or chain of mountains
8. A dry area with little or no vegetation
9. A narrow valley with high steep sides
10. A point of land that extends into a body of water
11. A high, steep wall of rock
12. An area of high, flat land with steep slopes on at least one side

## Bodies of Water

1. A small body of flowing water
2. A large ocean off the east coast of the Americas
3. Five major lakes shared by the United States and Canada
4. Major gulf found off the southern coast of the United States
5. This major U.S. river empties into the Gulf of Mexico in Louisiana.
6. The city of San Francisco is found on this bay.
7. This major river forms part of the border between the United States and Mexico.
8. Large area of water off Alaska's north coast
9. A small area of ocean partly surrounded by land
10. A waterway dug across land for transportation or irrigation
11. Place where a river or stream empties into a larger body of water

## Geographic Pinpoints

1. The most northern point on the earth
2. Large city found at the mouth of the Mississippi River
3. Major city located on Lake Michigan
4. The smallest state in the United States
5. Country that shares the northern border of the United States
6. Austin and Houston are found in this state.
7. The most southern point on the earth
8. Range of mountains that extends from Alabama to the Gulf of St. Lawrence
9. This cape is found near Boston.
10. Large city at the mouth of the Hudson River
11. The largest state in the United States
12. Alaska's capital city
13. Nation located south of the state of Arizona
14. Washington, D.C., is almost surrounded by this state.

**5**

**10**

©1978, 1988, 1997, 2002 Walch Publishing

11. An area of dense trees and plants with rain much of the year

12. A person who draws maps

13. Traveling from the mouth of a river to its source

14. Distance in degrees north and south of the equator

15. A large mass of slow-moving ice on a land surface

---

13. Silt built up at a river's mouth

14. Area between the Rocky Mountains and the Mississippi River

15. A point where a river forms a waterfall

16. Land area mostly surrounded by higher land

17. Plains bordered by large bodies of water

---

15. This state extends farther north than any other state in the United States.

16. Islands found off Florida's southern coast

17. The continental divide is located in this mountain range.

18. Range of mountains found in Washington and Oregon

19. California city found near the mouth of the Sacramento River

20. The largest of the Hawaiian Islands

---

12. An artificial lake where water is collected for use

13. This bay almost cuts the state of Maryland in half.

14. This major river joins the Mississippi River on the east and is the southern border of the state of Indiana.

15. Utah's largest lake

16. This large river forms part of the border between the states of Washington and Oregon.

17. This gulf lies off the southern coast of Alaska.

---

16. Areas containing large amounts of water, including marshes and swamps

17. Rolling land at the base of mountains

18. Large area of foothills east of the Appalachian Mountains

19. Lines of longitude are measured from this line.

20. Lines of latitude are also called this.

21. 66.5° north latitude

---

18. A narrow strip of land connecting two larger land areas

19. Broad, grassy area of plains

20. A broad plain in a polar area

21. A flat-topped hill with steep sides, usually in dry areas

22. Low, wet lands

---

18. A narrow waterway connecting two bodies of water

19. The deepest part of a waterway

20. A narrow inlet of the sea between high, steep banks

21. A river or stream that joins a larger river

22. This major U.S. river formed the Grand Canyon.

23. This canal connects the Hudson River and Lake Erie.

24. Large swamp/wetland area of Florida

25. This strait separates Alaska from Asia.

---

21. Island found off the coast of Connecticut

22. Mountain range north of the city of Anchorage

23. Desert found northeast of the city of Los Angeles

24. Area of highlands found in Arkansas

25. Cape found off the coast of North Carolina

---

NOTES

# The Exploration Period

## THOSE WHO DARED

1. Group of explorers who sailed from Norway, Iceland, or Greenland to North America about the year 1000
2. Queen who became interested in Columbus's plans to sail to the Indies
3. First European to discover the Pacific Ocean
4. Spaniard who conquered the Aztec Indians
5. First European to reach the mainland of North America
6. Name given to the first people of the Americas
7. First Englishman to sail around the world
8. French explorer who claimed the Mississippi Valley for France
9. Two French explorers who investigated the Mississippi River
10. French explorer who was the first European to discover the Gulf of St. Lawrence

## PLACES OF IMPORTANCE

1. Nation ruled in 1492 by Ferdinand and Isabella
2. Name given by Columbus to the island he landed upon
3. Country that paid for Columbus's voyage to the New World
4. Section of North America named by Ponce de Leon
5. Group of islands where Magellan was killed
6. Home of the Aztec Indians
7. Continent where the Inca Indians lived
8. Cape at the southern tip of Africa rounded by a Portuguese explorer in 1487
9. Area Columbus wanted to reach by sailing west
10. Island off the coast of North America named by John Cabot
11. South American country claimed by Cabral for Portugal

## THINGS IMPORTANT TO THE EXPLORERS

1. Metals the Spanish wanted from the New World
2. Columbus's three ships
3. Cloth the Europeans wanted from China
4. Settlement of people who left their own country for another land
5. Religion that Europeans wanted to spread to the New World
6. Determining a ship's direction and location and the distance it travels
7. A journey or voyage taken for a special reason
8. Home country of a colony
9. Animals released by Coronado's expedition
10. What Cortés brought along to Mexico to help him conquer the Aztec Indians

## GEOGRAPHIC PINPOINTS

1. Gulf explored and named by Cartier
2. Body of water Columbus sailed across to reach the New World
3. Magic water thought to fight aging
4. Narrow water passage
5. First name of the Pacific Ocean
6. De Soto was the first European to discover this river.
7. River explored by Cartier
8. River explored by Marquette and Joliet in the hope of finding the Northwest Passage
9. Body of water crossed by Vasco da Gama in his search for the New World
10. Ocean crossed by Magellan after he rounded Cape Horn

5

10

11. First Englishman to explore North America
12. Spanish explorer who was the first European to discover the Mississippi River
13. Spaniard who conquered the Inca Indians
14. Man who led an expedition from Cuba to Mexico in 1519
15. Portuguese explorer given credit for the first round-the-world voyage
16. Man who searched for the Fountain of Youth
17. First Spaniard to reach land that is now part of the United States
18. Spanish explorer and first European to see the Grand Canyon
19. Explorer who laid out the first French settlement in the New World
20. Portuguese explorer who claimed the west coast of North America for Spain
21. Portuguese explorer who was blown off course and gave Portugal claim to part of South America
22. Man sent by France to explore the east coast of North America

**15**

12. Group of islands in the New World, probably reached by Columbus
13. Country that financed Magellan's voyage
14. Country where the Inca Indians lived
15. First European country interested in discovering a new trade route to Asia
16. Name Columbus gave to an island south of Cuba
17. Two countries whose right to colonize the world was divided by the Line of Demarcation
18. Place Cortés used as his headquarters
19. Mountains Pizarro had to cross to get to Peru
20. Land over which Balboa walked to reach the Pacific Ocean
21. Seaport from which Columbus sailed for the Indies
22. Two of the countries where Columbus sought support for his trip to the Indies

**20**

11. Instrument that helped sailors tell directions
12. Disease caused by lack of fresh fruits and vegetables that killed many of Magellan's men
13. Imaginary line drawn by the pope to divide the world between Spain and Portugal
14. Columbus's flagship
15. Magellan's ship that survived to travel around the world
16. Sir Francis Drake's famous ship
17. Location hunted by many who explored the southwestern part of the United States
18. Route to Asia through North America sought by England and France
19. A daily record of a voyage or trip
20. A small Native American village or settlement in the American Southwest

11. Narrow body of water off the southern tip of South America that is named for an explorer
12. River where Hernando de Soto died and was buried
13. Body of water where Henry Hudson is thought to have died
14. Body of water that Sir Francis Drake thought was the western end of the Northwest Passage
15. Oceans that Sir Francis Drake sailed through on his trip around the world
16. Name given by the Vikings to the ocean they crossed
17. Excellent fishing area noted by explorers off the northeast coast of North America
18. The West Indies are located in this body of water.

NOTES

# The Colonial Period

## COLONIAL PERSONALITIES

1. Man who started the Roanoke Colony
2. Man who led the Jamestown Colony
3. Founder of Georgia
4. Man responsible for the settlement of Pennsylvania
5. Soldier who taught the Pilgrims how to defend themselves
6. Newspaperman thrown in jail for accusing his colony's governor of wrongdoing

7. Governor of Massachusetts Bay Colony
8. Two Native Americans who helped the Pilgrims survive
9. American Indian princess who is supposed to have saved John Smith's life
10. Minister who fled Massachusetts to start a colony that allowed religious freedom

## WHERE IN THE WORLD?

1. Island that was the site of England's first American colony
2. Colony settled by the Pilgrims
3. First permanent English colony in the New World
4. Cape first sighted by Plymouth settlers
5. Southernmost of the 13 English colonies
6. Colony in which Jamestown was located
7. Colony with the first form of representative government, the House of Burgesses

8. State in which Plymouth Colony was established
9. Colony settled by the Puritans
10. Colony whose proprietor was Lord Baltimore
11. European nation that controlled the city of Quebec
12. Dutch settlement in the New World
13. Island purchased for $24 by the Dutch
14. Swedish colony along the Delaware River

## ITEMS OF INTEREST

1. Metal sought by many Jamestown settlers
2. Ship that carried the Pilgrims to the New World
3. Insect that made many people in Jamestown ill
4. What the American Indians taught the Pilgrims to use on their crops as fertilizer
5. Occupation of most of the colonists in America
6. First major crop from Jamestown sold in England
7. Document that gave a group rights and privileges to settle an area

8. Word written on a post near the lost colony of Roanoke
9. Title held by George and Cecilius Calvert
10. Agreement the Pilgrims signed that gave them the beginnings of self-government
11. Resource desired by the French in building their empire in the New World
12. Intended reading matter for children who were taught to read and write
13. Two instruments used by New England colonists to punish wrongdoers

## COLONIAL IDEAS AND BELIEFS

1. Exchange of goods
2. What the Puritans and Pilgrims hoped to have in the New World
3. Form of government favored by most colonists, in which people rule themselves

4. State religion that made many English people decide to settle in America
5. Religion of most of the people who settled in Maryland
6. Idea that John Peter Zenger helped establish in America

5

10

*American History Challenge!* ©1978, 1988, 1997, 2002 Walch Publishing

7. Form of government practiced in Virginia, in which people elected other people to make laws for them

8. Major idea of the Mayflower Compact, which led to our democracy

9. Person like William Penn who works for the welfare of all

10. Kind of freedom first allowed in the colonies by Rhode Island

11. Refusal to accept a bill passed by a colonial legislature

12. Situation that existed in the colonies when religion and government were not under one control

13. Priests who hoped to convert American Indians to the Christian faith

14. Wooden paddle to which a single sheet of printed material was attached, used by children learning to read

15. Trading company that sent colonizers to Jamestown

16. First form of representative government in the New World

17. Act passed in 1649 to allow religious freedom in Maryland

18. Term for the first terrible winter in Jamestown

19. Hartford's written plan of government

20. Trade between Africa, the West Indies, and the New England colonies

21. Local self-government bodies in the New England colonies

22. Laws passed by the English to control trade

23. England's lawmaking body

24. Schoolbook used by the New England colonists to teach reading and writing

25. This drink made from the seed of the cacao tree was a favorite drink of the Aztecs.

15. This Spanish colony was the oldest city founded by Europeans in the United States.

16. Area formed in 1691 by the union of Massachusetts Bay and Plymouth colonies

17. City of Brotherly Love founded by Quaker colonizers

18. Site of the first Spanish colony west of the Mississippi River in what is now the United States

19. Country in which the Pilgrims had tried to live before coming to the New World

20. City once known as New Amsterdam

21. City and colony established by Thomas Hooker

22. City and colony settled by Roger Williams

23. Name of land area owned by Sir George Carteret and Lord Berkeley

24. Three geographical groups into which the 13 colonies were divided

25. Rich fishing area used by colonists off the coast of Newfoundland

11. King of England when Jamestown was established

12. Queen of England during the early colonial period

13. Man who learned how to produce tobacco

14. Second governor of Plymouth Colony

15. Leader of the Dutch colony who bought land from the American Indians for $24

16. First English child born in the New World

17. Dutch leader who told the Swedes to get off Dutch land

18. First governor of Plymouth Colony

19. Woman ordered to leave Massachusetts Bay Colony for expressing her ideas on religion

20. English king for whom North and South Carolina were named

21. Man who led a rebellion of Virginia farmers

22. Person chosen by a king or queen to rule a Spanish colony

15

20

NOTES

©1978, 1988, 1997, 2002 Walch Publishing

# Colonial Life

## WATER BODIES THE COLONISTS KNEW

1. Large body of water along which early settlements were started
2. Body of water between Boston and Cape Cod
3. Body of water the English settlers of the New World had to cross
4. River along which Williamsburg was established
5. River along which New York grew
6. Bay in Delaware on which colonies grew
7. River on which Hartford was established
8. Richest of all North American fishing waters, visited by colonial fishing vessels
9. Inlet of the Atlantic Ocean in Maryland and Virginia, explored by John Smith
10. Body of water lying between the states of New York and Vermont

## THINGS IMPORTANT TO THE COLONISTS

1. American Indian crop the settlers learned to grow
2. Boat that the American Indians showed the colonists how to make and use
3. Structure built to grind corn and wheat
4. Beast of burden brought by the colonists to the New World
5. Main occupation of colonists in New England until the mid-1800s
6. Main crop of Virginia, Maryland, and North Carolina
7. Making this taught a young girl both her sewing stitches and her letters
8. Plant grown in the Southern colonies and used in making dyes
9. Three of the four major crops of the Southern colonies
10. One of the major industries of the New England colonies
11. Kind of sap first collected by Native Americans
12. Kind of shoes first used by Native Americans to walk on snow

## SOMEWHERE IN THE NEW WORLD?

1. Colonies found along the northern Atlantic coast
2. Colonies that had more rain, longer summers, and richer land
3. Thinly settled area of forests and small farms just beyond the last settled community
4. Large southern farms
5. Uninhabited and uncultivated region
6. Country that many southern colonists bought goods from and traded goods to

## WHO LIVED IN THE NEW WORLD?

1. People who helped the colonists survive in the wilderness
2. People who shod horses and worked with metal
3. Term for a person who could train apprentices
4. People brought to the New World in 1619 to be sold to settlers
5. People who worked for a specified period of time in the New World in return for their passage
6. Only people allowed to attend schools in colonial times
7. Common name for Society of Friends, who settled in Pennsylvania
8. Workers skilled in making things
9. People who owned shops where they sold food, clothing, tools, and furniture
10. French Protestants who came to the colonies to escape their king

5

10

©1978, 1988, 1997, 2002 Walch Publishing

11. Body of water between Long Island and the southern New England colonies

12. Large bay on which Baltimore was established

13. River flowing into the Hudson that was named for a Native American tribe

14. Bay on which the colony of Providence was located

15. River along which the colony of Savannah was settled

16. Longest river in New England

17. Philadelphia was founded near the mouth of this river.

18. A low coastal plain full of waterways

---

13. Kind of Old World metal the colonists' tools were made of

14. Cloth the colonists made from sheep's hair

15. New England industry that became important during the 1700s

16. Kind of home first built by the Swedish settlers

17. Most important meat in the colonial diet

18. School attended by young Puritan children to learn their ABCs

19. Cloth the colonists made from flax

20. Tar, pitch, and turpentine

21. Taxes to be paid on goods sent to the colonies

22. Legislature to which voters elected representatives

23. Body of citizen-soldiers who met to train and defend their own colony

24. Crops produced in excess of what farm families could use

25. System used by England to control the trade of the colonies

---

7. Mountain range that lay directly west of the 13 colonies

8. Colonies that arose between the Hudson River and Delaware Bay

9. Island near the Grand Banks

10. New England town that became the greatest whaling seaport in the world

11. The center of a New England village

12. In a New England town, political business is conducted here.

13. Part of the coast of North Carolina is protected by this cape.

---

11. First colonizers of Delaware

12. Free people who came to Jamestown in 1619 to help the colony grow

13. People who did not want to separate from the Church of England but wanted to change it somewhat

14. Separatists who came to the New World to colonize

15. Nobles who founded colonies

16. People who made barrels and casks

17. Powerful Native American tribe of the New York area

18. New settlers who came to live in the colonies

19. A person directly responsible for field slaves

15

20

N O T E S

©1978, 1988, 1997, 2002 Walch Publishing

# The French and Indian War

## IMPORTANT PEOPLE

1. Man sent in 1753 to warn the French to get out of the Ohio River valley

2. Commander of British forces in America at the start of the war

3. Man who founded the settlement of Boonesborough

4. People who moved west to build their homes and settle the land

5. French general who defended Quebec

6. Man appointed to lead the British forces in America in the middle of the war

## IMPORTANT LOCATIONS ON LAND

1. Name given to the area of French control in the New World

2. Land claimed by both the English and the French, leading to the war

3. French fort at the head of the Ohio River

4. Area into which English settlers wanted to be allowed to move

5. Nation that controlled more land in the New World before than after the war

6. Oldest French settlement in the New World

7. Colony that was George Washington's birthplace

8. Name given to Fort Duquesne when it was captured by the British

9. State in which Boonesborough was located

10. Continent where England and France are found

## IMPORTANT THINGS AND IDEAS

1. Structures built to protect settlers who lived west of the Appalachian Mountains

2. Many settlers built these to live in.

3. Religion of England at the time of the war

4. Plan proposed by Benjamin Franklin for the common defense of the colonies

5. All lands west of the Mississippi River were claimed by this country after the French and Indian War.

6. Powder for muskets was kept in this.

## IMPORTANT LOCATIONS ON WATER

1. Major tributary of the Mississippi River that was claimed by both England and France

2. River that formed the western border of the English colonies after the war

3. Great Lake to the north of Fort Pitt

4. River whose tributaries include the Mohawk

5. Trade route controlled by the French-owned city of New Orleans

6. River in New York followed by colonists who were moving west

5

10

©1978, 1988, 1997, 2002 Walch Publishing

7. River along which Quebec is located

8. This body of water is north of Fort Niagara.

9. Rivers that meet to form the Ohio River

10. River down which the French traveled to supply Fort Duquesne

---

11. Great Lake out of which the St. Lawrence River flows

12. River that British troops sailed up to attack Quebec

13. Fort Ticonderoga was located on this body of water

---

7. Religion of France at the time of the war

8. What the British forces built before attacking Fort Duquesne

9. Geographic feature that helped in the defense of Quebec

---

10. Peace treaty that ended the war

11. Buildings used by the French to protect their widely scattered settlements

12. War that France and England fought in Europe at the same time as the French and Indian War

---

11. Natural barrier that had kept settlers out of the Ohio River valley

12. French fort on Cape Breton Island in Nova Scotia

13. City located where Fort Duquesne once stood

14. Nation given the city of New Orleans by the French in 1762

15. Territory given up by Spain at the end of the war

---

16. Site of the fighting for Quebec

17. Village in northwestern Massachusetts destroyed by the French and the Native Americans

18. European nation that helped France during the war

19. England, Scotland, and Wales

20. Fort built by George Washington and his men to protect them from the French

---

7. Leader of the British government in the middle of the war

8. Tribe of Native Americans that helped the English against the French in the war

9. King of France during the war

10. Friends who help in time of need

---

11. Man who proposed the first attempt to unite the American colonies

12. French general who died at the battle of Quebec

13. Governor of Virginia who sent Washington to tell the French to leave the Ohio Valley

14. Two Native American tribes that aided the French in the war

---

15

20

NOTES

©1978, 1988, 1997, 2002 Walch Publishing

# Steps Leading to Revolution

## INGREDIENTS OF THE REVOLUTION

1. Illegal goods brought into the colonies without being taxed
2. Committees organized to keep the colonies informed of events by writing letters
3. Slogan about taxes that influenced many colonists to rebel against Great Britain
4. Tax paid directly to the British government
5. War that the British paid for by raising the colonists' taxes

6. Form of government in which people elect other people to make laws for them
7. Refusal by the colonists to buy British goods
8. Group that drew up a list of complaints against the King of England
9. Colonial firearms
10. Goods brought into the colonies
11. Undisciplined groups of people who destroyed stamped papers to protest the Stamp Act

## ACTS AND LAWS

1. Act that required a tax on all written documents, making the colonists furious
2. Acts passed to punish the colonies for rebelling against the Stamp Act
3. Document that forbade English colonists from moving across the Appalachian Mountains
4. To have an act withdrawn or canceled

5. Act decreeing that Parliament had the right to pass whatever laws were needed to govern the empire
6. Acts declaring that tobacco, wool, cotton, sugar, and indigo could be sold only in England
7. Document that forced colonists in the Ohio River valley to move back to the original 13 colonies
8. Acts that required all goods to be shipped to and from the colonies on English ships

## IMPORTANT LOCATIONS

1. City where the famous "massacre" occurred
2. City where the first Continental Congress met
3. Colony in which Boston was located
4. City that had a "tea party"

5. Colony where the Stamp Act Congress met
6. Chain of mountains beyond which English colonists could not settle
7. Places where colonial troops first fired on British troops
8. Colony that seemed to take the lead in disobeying British laws

## MAKERS OF THE REVOLUTION

1. Man who began the ride to warn the colonists that the British were coming to Concord
2. King of England during the Revolution
3. Patriots who dressed as Native Americans and dumped tea into Boston Harbor
4. Slang term for a British soldier
5. Name given to colonial soldiers who could be ready to fight quickly

6. Man who said, "Give me liberty or give me death."
7. British general who controlled Boston under the Intolerable Acts
8. Leader of the Sons of Liberty in Massachusetts
9. The colonists in North America
10. Colonists who were loyal to the British government

5

10

©1978, 1988, 1997, 2002 Walch Publishing

12. Colonial legislature in Virginia
13. Lawmaking body of England
14. Tax on goods imported into the colonies
15. Formal request sent to the king
16. Punishment used by colonists against supporters of England
17. Native American uprising in the Ohio River valley after the French and Indian War

18. Goods that could be sold only in England
19. Special search warrants carried by "officers of the crown" when they searched colonial homes
20. Commodity that continued to be taxed after the Townshend Acts were repealed
21. Trading company that brought tea to the colonies
22. One company with complete control over a product or service
23. Harsh and unjust rule

9. Harsh laws passed to punish the people of Boston
10. Act passed by the First Continental Congress in which colonial rights were listed
11. Act that permitted the French in Canada to follow their religion and control their schools

12. Law that required the colonists to provide barracks and supplies for British troops in America
13. Law that abolished Virginia's elected House of Burgesses
14. These colonists united and developed a statement of rights

9. British soldiers were quartered or housed here.
10. Samuel Adams lived in this colony.
11. Colony where Patrick Henry lived
12. Town in which Samuel Adams and John Hancock hid from General Gage

13. Colony whose assembly was forbidden to meet by the Townshend Acts
14. Colony in which the towns of Lexington and Concord were located
15. Paul Revere crossed this river to get from Boston to Charlestown.
16. First city to decide not to import goods from Great Britain

11. Boston lawyer who organized the Committees of Correspondence
12. Ottawa chief who organized the Native Americans against the English colonists
13. Colonial lawyer who defended the English soldiers after the Boston Massacre
14. Man who completed the ride to warn the people of Concord that the British were coming
15. Virginian who was a powerful speaker against unpopular British acts

16. Englishman who became Chancellor of the Exchequer and was responsible for the Stamp Act
17. Boston lawyer who proposed the Stamp Act Congress
18. The African-American colonist killed at the Boston Massacre
19. Samuel Adams and this man were to be arrested by the British in Lexington.

**15**

**20**

NOTES

# The American Revolution

## FAMOUS QUOTATIONS

1. "Give me liberty or give me death."
2. "We must all hang together or assuredly we shall all hang separately."
3. "I only regret that I have but one life to lose for my country."
4. "I have not yet begun to fight."
5. "These are the times that try men's souls."
6. This man wrote to his wife, Martha, that he hoped his "going would answer some good purpose."
7. "When in the course of human events, it becomes necessary for one people to dissolve the political bands which have connected them with another . . ."
8. "I am not a Virginian but an American."

## IMPORTANT ELEMENTS

1. Document that explains why the colonies had to separate from England
2. England's lawmaking body
3. Complete freedom from Britain meant this.
4. This is a signal that means one side wants to surrender.
5. Group that acted as the government for the colonies during the Revolution
6. Pamphlet written by Thomas Paine that influenced many people to favor the split with England
7. Protective walls of dirt and stone
8. John Paul Jones's ship

## IMPORTANT LOCATIONS

1. Body of water on the eastern border of the colonies
2. European country that helped the Americans win the Revolution
3. Place where George Washington and the colonial troops spent a miserable winter
4. Name of George Washington's Virginia plantation
5. City in which the peace conference to end the Revolution was held
6. Colony in which Valley Forge was located
7. Site of the battle known as the turning point of the Revolution
8. Two cities in Canada that Benedict Arnold fought to capture
9. Body of water crossed by Washington and his troops to attack the British at Trenton
10. Nation's western border after the Revolution
11. Bay on which Yorktown was located
12. Bodies of water that formed the nation's northern border after the Revolution

## PEOPLE OF THE REVOLUTION

1. Man chosen to lead the Continental Army
2. King of England during the American Revolution
3. German troops in America
4. People who opposed the split with England
5. American general in charge of West Point who became a traitor
6. Man given credit for forming the American navy
7. General called the Swamp Fox
8. Commander who surrendered the British troops at Yorktown
9. British general who failed to meet Burgoyne and Howe at Saratoga because he had been beaten at Oriskany
10. Man in charge of training troops at Valley Forge
11. General nicknamed Gentleman Johnny
12. Leader of the Green Mountain Boys
13. One of Washington's best generals in North Carolina
14. Leader of American troops in the area north of the Ohio River
15. Frenchman who was Washington's trusted aide

**5**

**10**

©1978, 1988, 1997, 2002 Walch Publishing

©1978, 1988, 1997, 2002 Walch Publishing

9. "Even peace may be purchased at too high a price."

10. "We hold these truths to be self-evident, that all men are created equal . . ."

11. "Don't fire until you see the whites of their eyes."

12. "We fight, get beat, rise, and fight again."

13. "With a heart full of love and gratitude, I now take my leave of you."

14. "I retire from the great theater of action."

15. "Those who would give up essential liberty to purchase a little temporary safety deserve neither liberty nor safety."

16. "These united Colonies are, and of right ought to be, free and independent states."

9. What Patriots often covered loyalists with

10. Closing off of the Atlantic Coast by ships

11. Ship defeated by the *Bonhomme Richard*

12. Weapons captured from Fort Ticonderoga and used against the British in Boston

13. Armed merchant ships

14. Wartime colonial money that inspired the phrase "not worth a . . ."

15. Book for which the *Bonhomme Richard* was named

16. Petition sent to the king to stop the war

13. Bay that divided the colony of Maryland

14. Fort on the Wabash River captured by George Rogers Clark and his men

15. Colony that was the birthplace of Thomas Jefferson

16. Nation that sent troops to help the British fight the Americans

17. City where the Second Continental Congress met

18. Place where the Battle of Bunker Hill was actually fought

19. City where the Battle of Bunker Hill took place

20. Two forts on Lake Champlain captured by Burgoyne

21. Land area lost by Britain to Spain at the end of the Revolution

22. Body of water on which Ticonderoga and Crown Point were situated

23. River on which West Point was located

24. Canadian body of water for which America received fishing rights as a provision of the peace treaty

16. American ambassador to France during the Revolution

17. Author of most of the Declaration of Independence

18. Author of a pamphlet on the colonists' duty to rebel against England

19. Man in charge of colonial troops at Bunker Hill

20. General who controlled the British forces in Boston after Bunker Hill

21. Colonist who first proposed separation from England before the Continental Congress

22. Leader of the American forces that captured Montreal

23. General who replaced Howe as leader of the British forces

24. Two Polish officers who served in the American army

25. British general who surrendered his forces at Saratoga

26. Woman who became famous during the Battle of Monmouth when she replaced her wounded husband as gunner

27. King of France who agreed to help the Americans in their fight

**15**

**20**

NOTES

## GOVERNMENT OF THE PEOPLE

1. Elderly Pennsylvania delegate sent to the meeting to revise the Articles of Confederation
2. Man chosen to be the nation's first president
3. Man who proposed the idea of the Bill of Rights
4. Washington's secretary of the treasury
5. Washington's secretary of state
6. Second president of the United States
7. Man appointed by John Adams to be Chief Justice of the Supreme Court
8. Washington's secretary of war
9. Man chosen to be the first vice president
10. Lawmakers elected for two-year terms
11. Virginian called the Father of the Constitution
12. Man who represented the United States in France when the Articles of Confederation were being revised
13. Lawmakers elected for six-year terms

## IMPORTANT LOCATIONS

1. Body of water that separates Europe and the United States
2. Bodies of water used by many farmers to get their goods to market
3. George Washington's home
4. Site of the meeting to revise the Articles of Confederation
5. Washington's birthplace
6. Ninth state to ratify the Constitution, putting it into force
7. First state to ratify the Constitution
8. Country that had a revolution shortly after the U.S. government was established
9. City that controlled trade up and down the Mississippi River
10. Large body of salt water near New Orleans
11. River that starts at Pittsburgh and joins the Mississippi

## THE TRAPPINGS OF GOVERNMENT

1. First written form of American government
2. Important law of 1787 that organized the lands north of the Ohio River
3. Lawmaking body of the United States
4. First 10 amendments to the Constitution
5. Presidential advisory group first formed by President Washington
6. What D.C. stands for in Washington, D.C.
7. Hamilton's excise tax that made western farmers angry
8. New political party led by Alexander Hamilton
9. Political party led by Thomas Jefferson
10. Under the Articles of Confederation, the number of states that had to agree to pass a law
11. What colonial assemblies became in the new state governments
12. Series of papers written to support the new federal government

## THE GOVERNMENT'S IDEAS AND POWERS

1. Changes or additions to the Constitution
2. System under which each branch of government keeps the other two from becoming too strong
3. Rejection by the president of a bill
4. Basic weakness of government under the Articles of Confederation
5. Power that the Central Congress lacked under the Articles of Confederation
6. Plan proposed at the Constitutional Convention to give more power to the large states
7. Approval of the new government by the 13 states
8. Settlement reached when opposing sides give in to get agreement

**5**

**10**

©1978, 1988, 1997, 2002 Walch Publishing

9. Tax on goods brought into a country

10. Washington's proposal of noninvolvement in the quarrels of Europe

11. Plan proposed by the small states at the Constitutional Convention

12. Union of states or nations

13. Under this government, Congress had no means of solving the nation's money problems.

14. Right to unload ships and store goods on the docks

15. A form of government in which the people elect representatives

16. When powers are shared between states and a national government

13. Term for a mile square under the Northwest Ordinance

14. House of Congress in which each state is represented according to its population

15. Branch of government that includes the president and his Cabinet

16. Document that contains the supreme law of the land

17. House of Congress in which each state is allowed two votes

18. Number of states needed to change the Articles of Confederation

19. Branch of government formed to settle quarrels between the states

20. Treaty in which Great Britain agreed with the United States to get out of the Northwest Territory

21. National governing body under the Articles of Confederation

22. Under the Northwest Ordinance, a six-mile-square piece of land

23. What one section of each township was set aside to support

24. The three branches of the federal government

12. River along which Washington, D.C., is located

13. River that forms the border between Maryland and Virginia

14. The land north of the Ohio River was called this

15. James Madison was elected to Congress from this state

16. River that forms the border between South Carolina and Georgia

17. Colony that refused to agree to the new form of government unless the other colonies gave up their claims to western lands

18. Two states that did not ratify the Constitution in time to vote in the first national election

19. Site of meeting called by Virginia to discuss the Articles of Confederation

20. Country that controlled the city of New Orleans

21. State that did not send a delegate to the convention to revise the Articles of Confederation

22. When Ben Franklin was 81, he was governor of this state.

14. Man who represented the United States in England when the Articles of Confederation were being revised

15. Patriot from Virginia who fought against the Constitution

16. Man who invented the township method of surveying land

17. Leader of the farmers' revolt against lawsuits that were taking their farms

18. Man whose notes tell us much of what happened at the Constitutional Convention

19. Three men who wrote the *Federalist Papers*

20. Only man to sign the Declaration of Independence, the Articles of Confederation, and the Constitution

21. Man who worked out the agreement between the United States and Spain for President Washington

22. French diplomat who tried to get the United States to side with France against Great Britain

**15**

**20**

N O T E S

©1978, 1988, 1997, 2002 Walch Publishing

# Testing the New Government

**10**

## IMPORTANT PEOPLE

1. First secretary of the treasury

2. First secretary of state

3. First president of the United States

4. First Chief Justice of the new Supreme Court

5. Second president of the United States

6. Man who refused to serve more than two terms as president

7. This man was the first vice president.

8. Man who challenged Jefferson for the presidency, making it necessary for the House to decide the issue

9. Three ministers who met with U.S. commissioners in France

10. Leader of the Federalists who wanted the national government to be stronger than the state governments

## IMPORTANT LOCATIONS

1. River on which the country's capital was built

2. Two states that gave land for the new capital

3. Place to which George Washington retired

4. Name given to the capital city of the United States

5. City in which the Bank of the United States was located

6. Name of the federal district in which the capital was located

## AFFAIRS OF THE NEW GOVERNMENT

1. Political party to which John Adams belonged

2. List of American freedoms

3. The first 10 amendments to the Constitution

4. Body that chooses the president when no one has a majority of electoral votes

5. What France demanded before it would talk to U.S. ministers

6. Entity given power by the Constitution to borrow money

7. Certificates given to people who had loaned money to the federal government during the Revolution

8. Beverage that caused a rebellion when it was taxed by the federal government

## CONCEPTS IMPORTANT TO THE NEW GOVERNMENT

1. Person who runs for office

2. Money owed

3. Selection of a person to run for office

4. Being installed in office as the president

5. Capturing American sailors and forcing them to serve in the British navy

6. Source of money for operation of the government

**5**

**10**

©1978, 1988, 1997, 2002 Walch Publishing

7. Not taking sides in an argument

8. Supporters of Alexander Hamilton's ideas

9. Tax placed on goods made within a country

---

10. Government's promise to repay the money it is loaned

11. Tax on goods imported into a nation

12. Action that brings on public disorder or that leads to treason

13. Group of citizens who tend to think alike about money problems and who influence the government's actions

---

9. Organization established by the federal government to issue paper money called bank notes

10. Plan to pay the states' debts

11. Treaty by which Great Britain agreed to get out of the area west of the Appalachian Mountains

12. Agreement in 1800 between the United States and France

---

13. Act that gave the president power to deport foreigners living in the United States

14. Acts passed during Adams's term that threatened the freedom of speech and press

15. Jefferson's political party

---

7. State in which the Whiskey Rebellion occurred

8. Place where the new national coins were made

9. Nation with which the United States fought an undeclared war in the 1790s

---

10. Nation that still held forts in the area between the Appalachian Mountains and the Mississippi River

11. Former ally that caused difficulties for President Adams

12. The President's Palace is now called this

---

11. Diplomat sent by Washington to Great Britain to work out a treaty

12. Leader who favored a policy of neutrality

13. Man whose goal in the first government was to make the government financially sound

14. Leader who believed that state governments should be strong because they were close to the people

---

15. Frenchman sent to try to get the United States to fight Great Britain

16. Two men who were heads of the first political parties

17. Third president of the United States

18. Man who worked to help Jefferson get elected by the House of Representatives

---

**15**

**20**

NOTES

# Politics

## PEOPLE IN POLITICS

1. Person who takes over when something happens to the U.S. president
2. Person who heads a state's government
3. Person who heads a city's government
4. People who hold public offices
5. Person who heads the U.S. government

6. Person who tries to be elected
7. Person who heads the U.S. Senate
8. Head of the Supreme Court
9. Person who casts a ballot
10. Ruler with complete power over a country

## PLACES OF POLITICAL IMPORTANCE

1. Capital of the United States
2. This was set up by Congress to handle correspondence between people.
3. This is what D.C. stands for in Washington, D.C.

4. Washington, D.C., is located on this river.
5. House of Congress that must approve a presidential appointment
6. Term of office for this part of government is two years.

## POLITICAL CONCEPTS

1. More than half of a group
2. To express disapproval, to object, or to dissent
3. Less than half of a group
4. True or false information designed to make people believe ideas
5. Pardon for a wrong done against a government
6. Power to reject an act or a bill

7. Strong feelings of loyalty and patriotism toward your nation
8. System in which one branch of government limits the power of the other two
9. To compel observance of a law
10. Decision reached when both sides give in a little
11. Rights given to the citizens of a country by their government
12. To choose leaders by votes

## POLITICAL THINGS

1. Document on which the U.S. government is based
2. People who listen to court cases and decide the guilt or innocence of the accused
3. Public meeting to express people's feelings or views
4. Central or national government of the United States
5. Rule made by a government to be used in governing its people

6. Branch of government that includes the president, vice president, and Cabinet
7. Personal freedoms listed in the Constitution are found here.
8. Body representing the legislative branch of the U.S. government
9. Agreement between nations
10. National lawmaking body of the United States
11. Written request sent to someone in public office

5

10

©1978, 1988, 1997, 2002 Walch Publishing

©1978, 1988, 1997, 2002 Walch Publishing

12. Place in which arrested people are tried
13. Additions to the Constitution
14. Document that lists personal freedoms of the people of the United States
15. Things a person must have before running for office
16. Length of time a president is in office is called this.

17. Survey made by asking many people the same questions and studying the answers
18. Gathering of people for some purpose, such as a discussion of who will run for an office
19. Only amendment to the U.S. Constitution to have been repealed
20. Body representing the judicial branch of the U.S. government
21. To serve in this part of the federal government, a person must be at least thirty years old.

13. Government run by the people
14. The trial to remove an elected official is called this.
15. Claim that authority to rule comes directly from God
16. Power that is unlimited or unquestioned
17. To cancel or annul a law
18. To forbid by law or by an order

19. System of government based on the idea of public ownership of land and capital
20. Right to vote
21. To accept a bill and sign it into law
22. Incorporation of individuals of different races as equals into society
23. Interference of one party or nation in the affairs of another to protect its own interests

7. States that gave the land on which Washington, D.C., became situated
8. Building that houses the Senate and the House of Representatives
9. Official residence of the president

10. House of Congress in which money bills must start
11. Official residence of the vice president
12. The power to declare war is given to this part of government.

11. Group of people elected to make laws and manage a town or city
12. Head of a monarchy
13. U.S. lawmakers elected for two years
14. Person who studies how people govern themselves
15. Commander in chief of the U.S. armed forces

16. First nonelected president of the United States
17. U.S. lawmakers elected for six years
18. People who worked for voting rights for women
19. Person who tries to influence the votes of lawmakers
20. Person (other than the president) in charge of affairs
21. Person who heads the House of Representatives

**15**

**20**

NOTES

# The War of 1812 and an Expanding Nation

## EVENTS AND POLICIES

1. Policy declaring that the American continent was no longer open for European colonization

2. "Mr. Madison's War"

3. Two European nations that were often at war, which led to the War of 1812

4. Practice of rewarding members of the winning party in an election with government jobs

## WAR ON THE WATER

1. U.S. ship nicknamed "Old Ironsides"

2. This nation had the strongest navy in the world in 1812.

3. Some of the most important battles during the War of 1812 occurred on these bodies of water.

4. Act of taking American sailors from their ships and making them serve on British ships

5. Theory that all nations should be able to use the oceans without restrictions from other countries

## SITES OF ACTION

1. Nation from which the United States bought the Louisiana Territory

2. City burned by the British when they landed in Maryland during the War of 1812

3. Body of water that formed the eastern boundary of the Louisiana Territory

4. Large body of water along which the city of New Orleans lies

5. British area in North America desired by the War Hawks

6. Canadian capital that burned in the War of 1812

7. Site of the British attack during which "The Star-Spangled Banner" was written

8. Nation that controlled Florida during the War of 1812

9. Starting point of Lewis and Clark's journey to explore the Louisiana Territory

10. Colorado mountain named for Zebulon Pike

11. Early explorer's name for the Great Plains

12. Body of water between Canada and the United States where the American navy defeated the British

## IMPORTANT PEOPLE

1. U.S. president when the Louisiana Territory was added to the United States

2. Two men who led the expedition to explore the Louisiana Territory

3. Group of men in Congress who wanted a second war with England

4. Man who wrote "The Star-Spangled Banner"

5. Native American woman who helped Lewis and Clark

6. People who moved west to settle new lands

7. One of the first pioneers to cross the Appalachian Mountains into Kentucky

8. Leader of France who sold the Louisiana Territory to the United States

9. Fourth president of the United States

10. Native American chief who tried to organize the Native Americans against the white settlers in 1810

11. Two men who led the War Hawks

12. Naval officer who controlled American ships on Lake Erie

**5**

**10**

©1978, 1988, 1997, 2002 Walch Publishing

5. Policy by which some nations tried not to take sides in the War of 1812

6. An area that separates settled land from wilderness

7. Political party whose members did not generally favor the War of 1812

8. Agreement that brought an official end to the War of 1812

9. This act of nature helped cause the British to retreat from Washington.

6. Vessels that the British Orders in Council said must be stopped and examined by the British

7. U.S. ship fired on by the British in 1807

8. British ships captured by the American navy and by privateers

9. Tactic used by England and France during the war between them to prevent ships from entering each other's harbors

10. Law nicknamed the O-Grab-Me Act

13. An important pass through the Appalachian Mountains

14. The city of Baltimore was defended by this fort.

15. Body of water on which Captain Thomas Macdonough defeated four British ships

16. Region of the United States that generally did not favor the War of 1812

17. Name by which Fort Dearborn was later known

18. Fort in the upper Great Lakes region that fell to the British in the War of 1812

19. State from which Henry Clay came

20. Territory that was added to the United States in 1819 after Andrew Jackson had taken troops to control the American Indians there

21. State that John C. Calhoun represented in Congress

22. City where the treaty ending the War of 1812 was signed

23. River followed by Lewis and Clark to the Pacific Ocean

13. Commander of U.S. troops in New Orleans

14. President during the Era of Good Feelings

15. This man was president during the War of 1812.

16. Leader of an expedition into the northern part of the Louisiana Territory

17. Head of the American Fur Company

18. Mountain man who discovered South Pass through the Rocky Mountains in Wyoming

19. Man who defeated Tecumseh at the Battle of Tippecanoe

20. Two men who arranged the purchase of the Louisiana Territory

21. Woman said to have saved the Declaration of Independence when the city of Washington burned

22. U.S. general known as Old Hickory

23. American who won a naval victory on Lake Champlain in 1814

24. This senator from Kentucky wanted the Native American treaties honored.

15

20

NOTES

# The Mexican War and Westward Expansion

## POLITICAL EVENTS AND IDEAS

1. Institution opposed by many people, especially in the North

2. What Texas was for nine years before it became a state

3. Battle cry of Texans in 1836

4. Religion of Mexico, disliked by many Texans

5. An object that indicates surrender

6. Series of laws that admitted California to the Union as a free state

## WESTWARD EXPANSION

1. Form of transportation for which a southern route was needed, prompting U.S. purchase of Mexican land in 1853

2. Metal whose discovery caused many people to hurry to California

3. Path followed by settlers going to the Northwest

4. Groups of settlers traveling west together for protection

5. Vehicle that carried many people west

6. Grants that gave Americans permission to settle in certain areas

## PLACES AMERICANS WENT

1. Nation that welcomed settlers from the United States after winning its independence from Spain

2. Mission in San Antonio where many Texans died

3. Area in which American settlements led to problems with Mexico

4. Area referred to by the slogan "54-40 or Fight"

5. The Lone Star Republic

6. Body of water that forms California's western border

7. City in which 182 Texans died in a battle in 1836

8. Western state in which the Mormons settled

9. Large body of water in Utah

10. River that the United States wanted as a border between Texas and Mexico

11. Body of water crossed by Winfield Scott on his way to attack Veracruz

12. The Bear Flag Republic

## NAMES AMERICANS KNEW

1. U.S. president who tried to buy land from Mexico

2. American general who led U.S. forces into northern Mexico

3. Gold seekers who went to California

4. Man who received a land grant from Mexico and led people to settle in Texas

5. Leader of American troops in central Mexico

6. This man's discovery of gold in California started a gold rush.

7. Mormon leader who brought his people west

8. Man who started the Mormon religion

9. Dictator of Mexico during the Texans' war with Mexico

10. Texan who defeated Santa Anna's army at San Jacinto

11. Man who arranged in 1853 to buy 29,640 square miles of land from Mexico

12. This man owned a sawmill in California at which gold was discovered.

5

10

©1978, 1988, 1997, 2002 Walch Publishing

**7.** Name given to California's revolt against Mexico

**8.** Treaty that ended the Mexican War

**9.** Law passed by Mexico in 1830 that angered the United States

---

**7.** Idea that God wanted the United States to govern the land to the Pacific

**8.** System of bringing water to crops in ditches or canals, used by many farmers in the West

**9.** Purchase from Mexico that completed the area of the 48 states

---

**10.** Amendment introduced by David Wilmot to stop the spread of slavery

**11.** Political party to which Zachary Taylor belonged

**12.** Term that meant the citizens of a territory could decide the question of slavery

**13.** Term given to the block of land the United States got from Mexico at the close of the Mexican War

---

**10.** Extremely fast sailing ships that took people to California

**11.** Invention for which Jim Bowie is remembered

**12.** This city was called the Gateway to the West.

---

**13.** Place where Santa Anna suffered a major defeat in 1836

**14.** Site of General Scott's first major victory of the war

**15.** Country that controlled Texas and gave permission to Moses Austin for Americans to settle there

**16.** Final major battle that gave Americans control of northern Mexico

**17.** Area claimed by Britain, Spain, Russia, and the United States

**18.** River that Mexico wanted as the southern border of the United States

---

**19.** River that formed the northern border of the Gadsden Purchase

**20.** Rivers that bounded early American settlements in Texas

**21.** City outside of which the Battle of Chapultepec occurred

**22.** Place where the treaty to end the Mexican War was signed

**23.** River the Oregon Trail followed after leaving St. Louis

**24.** River the Oregon Trail followed until it joined the Columbia

---

**13.** This man's life was spared because he agreed that Texas should become independent.

**14.** Army officer who captured the area of New Mexico

**15.** General nicknamed Old Fuss and Feathers

**16.** Army officer called Pathfinder

**17.** General nicknamed Old Rough and Ready

**18.** Man sent to Mexico in 1845 in an attempt to buy land

---

**19.** Texan who commanded the Americans at the Alamo

**20.** Man who received permission in 1820 for Americans to settle in Texas

**21.** Negotiator of the treaty to end the Mexican War

**22.** Two famous frontiersmen who died at the Alamo

**23.** Group of pioneers trapped in the Sierra Nevada range by winter snow

**24.** Among the first missionaries to go west, they established a mission in the Walla Walla Valley.

---

**15**

**20**

NOTES

# Science and Inventions

| INVENTORS AND INVENTIONS | IMPORTANT LOCATIONS | TRANSPORTATION AND COMMUNICATION | INDUSTRIAL GROWTH |
|---|---|---|---|

**INVENTORS AND INVENTIONS**

1. Inventor of the cotton gin

2. Englishman who perfected the steam engine

3. Man given credit for the first successful steamboat

4. Immigrant who brought the secret of England's textile machines to the United States

5. Man who demonstrated the possibility of using interchangeable parts by assembling guns from a pile of parts

6. Maker of a six-shooter with a bullet chamber that spun into line with a fixed barrel

7. Inventor of a horse-drawn reaper that cut grain faster

8. Designer of clipper ships

9. Man who built the first efficient sewing machine driven by a foot treadle

10. Governor of New York who worked to establish the Erie Canal

**IMPORTANT LOCATIONS**

1. Kind of community to which people began moving to be near their work

2. Poor or run-down sections that developed in cities

3. Section of the nation that welcomed the invention of the cotton gin

4. This connected Lake Erie and the Hudson River.

5. Country in which the Industrial Revolution began

6. Sources of power along which early factories were located

7. Area that became a state in 1850, causing communication and transportation problems for the nation

8. River that the Erie Canal followed

**TRANSPORTATION AND COMMUNICATION**

1. "Fulton's Folly"

2. Means of sending messages using the telegraph

3. For many years, the principal means of travel within the United States

4. Means by which mail was carried rapidly from Missouri to Oregon or California in 1860

5. Great rafts used to float farm goods to market

6. Artificial waterway that connected the Hudson River and Lake Erie

7. Fee charged to use many roads in the 1800s

8. Name given to the first steam locomotive

9. Large canvas-covered wagons used for moving west

10. Person who "read" the river and navigated ships from place to place

**INDUSTRIAL GROWTH**

1. Place where workers make a product

2. The first important factories in the United States

3. Most of the work on the Southern plantations was done by these people.

4. Term that describes the drastic change during the 1800s in the way things were produced and distributed

5. Machines that make parts for other machines

6. Machine that harvests grain crops and separates the grain from the stalk

14

5

10

©1978, 1988, 1997, 2002 Walch Publishing

7. When a section of the country or a person spends most of the time doing one job or thing

8. Process in which interchangeable parts allowed huge amounts of goods to be produced

9. People who came to the United States to work in factories

10. Eli Whitney's idea: a series of parts that would fit any model of a given product

11. War that spurred the growth of American manufacturing

12. Using tools and knowledge to improve conditions

11. Nickname for the Erie Canal

12. Path that followed along the banks of the Erie Canal

13. Invention that brought an end to the Pony Express after only 18 months

14. Mechanisms built to raise or lower boats in a canal from one level to another

15. Steamship that surprised the world when it sailed across the Atlantic

16. Device on the front of locomotives to protect against stray cattle and buffalos

17. Device that allowed messages to travel rapidly between Europe and the United States

18. Donald McKay's extremely fast clipper ship

19. Activity for which a post road was used

20. Fastest sailing ships ever built

9. City in Missouri where the Pony Express and the Overland Mail started

10. Section of the United States where most of the early factories were found

11. The Wilderness Road went through this pass in the Appalachian Mountains.

12. Two cities joined by the first telegraph line

13. State that boasted the first water-powered textile factory in the country

14. City in New York that was the *Clermont's* first destination

15. Two cities that were connected by the Erie Canal

16. River on which the *Clermont* was first seen

11. Designer and builder of the first practical steam locomotive

12. Man who thought of dots and dashes to convey messages across telegraph wires

13. Frontiersman who cut the Wilderness Road into Kentucky

14. Man responsible for laying the Atlantic cable

15. Man concerned with the Overland Mail

16. Inventor of the sewing machine

17. Man who improved farming by making plowshares out of steel instead of cast iron

18. Man who accidentally discovered that heating rubber makes it more useful

19. Man who made his fortune with steamships and went on to control the New York Central Railroad

20. First American to sail around the earth

21. Man who developed a new factory where spinning, dyeing, and weaving were together in one building

15

20

N O T E S

©1978, 1988, 1997, 2002 Walch Publishing

# Prelude to the Civil War

## IMPORTANT PEOPLE

1. Man who invented the cotton gin, making slavery more profitable
2. Famous congressman from Kentucky nicknamed the Great Compromiser
3. Great politician from South Carolina
4. People who believed that slavery should be wiped out immediately
5. Man who debated with Stephen Douglas for the Senate seat from Illinois
6. Man who led an attack on Harpers Ferry to get guns for a slave uprising

7. Man elected president in 1860
8. Man who became president of the Confederacy
9. Author of *Uncle Tom's Cabin*
10. Man responsible for the Compromise of 1820
11. African-American woman who helped many slaves escape
12. African-American man who had his case heard by the Supreme Court

## IMPORTANT LOCATIONS

1. Section of the United States that became a leader in manufacturing and commerce
2. Area seeking statehood that was the subject of Henry Clay's first compromise
3. First Southern state to leave the Union
4. Site of first battle between North and South
5. Capital of the Confederacy after all the Southern states had left the Union

6. Many escaping slaves used this to guide them to freedom when they traveled at night
7. Country north of the United States which was the goal of many escaping slaves
8. Area that became a free state when Missouri became a slave state in 1820
9. Henry Clay's home state
10. Nation of freed slaves started by the American Colonization Society

## BACKGROUND FACTORS

1. Major crop of the Southern colonies prior to the Civil War
2. Probable major cause of the Civil War
3. Large Southern farms
4. Famous antislavery book written by Harriet Beecher Stowe
5. New nation formed by the Southern states

6. Occupation of Abe Lincoln before he became president
7. Tax on goods brought into the country from foreign lands
8. Paper printed by William Lloyd Garrison
9. Agreement that ended the slave trade in Washington, D.C.
10. Laws passed by each state listing things slaves were not allowed to do

## BACKGROUND IDEAS

1. Settlement reached when two arguing groups agree to give up some things
2. Prohibition of slavery
3. Area or state that did not allow slavery
4. When opposing groups of the same country fight a war

5. Idea that states should have the final say on matters that affect their citizens
6. Withdrawal of states from the Union
7. Nickname for Henry Clay
8. Nickname for Kansas in the period before the war

**5**

**10**

©1978, 1988, 1997, 2002 Walch Publishing

9. Nickname given to Stephen A. Douglas because of his size

10. Slave on the run

11. Taking the oath of office as a president

12. Idea that a state could outlaw or refuse to obey a law passed by Congress

13. Idea that the people in the area of the Mexican Cession should vote to decide whether their state would be slave or free

14. Slaves were considered this by their owners.

15. A formal argument between two sides to prove a point

11. Act that organized two new territories in the northern part of the Louisiana Purchase

12. Political party formed in 1854

13. Network of secret routes taken by escaped slaves through the North to Canada

14. Newspaper started by Frederick Douglass

15. Group that raised money and founded a colony in Africa for former slaves

16. Southerners' name for the extremely high tariff of 1828

17. Bill that said slavery should be forbidden in all lands taken from Mexico

18. Supreme Court case that tried to settle the slavery question

11. Area into which many Southerners wanted to extend slavery

12. National legislative body whose balance of power was a source of concern for both the North and the South

13. Area that wanted to enter the Union in 1850, resulting in another compromise

14. State that became angry about the Tariff of 1828 and threatened to leave the Union

15. Site of a famous raid on a federal arsenal

16. Area flooded by new Northern and Southern voters when it sought statehood

17. State in which Fort Sumter was located

18. Safe hiding places on the Underground Railroad

19. State Jefferson Davis was from

20. Free-state capital of Kansas

21. Site of raid led by John Brown in which five pro-slavery men were killed

22. Slave-state capital of Kansas

23. First capital of the Confederate States

13. Man who said, "A house divided against itself cannot stand."

14. Two men who debated the issue of states' rights in the Senate in 1830

15. Slave who escaped from Maryland and became a famous abolitionist

16. Illinois senator who proposed the Kansas-Nebraska Act

17. Leader of a raid in Kansas that killed five pro-slavery men

18. Harriet Tubman's nickname

19. Confederate general who attacked Fort Sumter

20. Man who ran for president in 1856 on the slogan "Free soil, free labor . . . and free men."

21. Supreme Court Chief Justice during the *Dred Scott* case

22. Black preacher who led a slave revolt in Virginia in 1831

23. Man who ran for the presidency in 1860 on the Southern Democratic ticket

15

20

NOTES

## AMERICANS AT WAR

1. President of the United States during the Civil War
2. Nickname given to Abraham Lincoln to describe his character
3. People who hated slavery and wanted to do away with it
4. Major military leader of the Southern forces
5. Northern general who received the Confederate surrender at Appomattox Courthouse
6. Assassin of President Lincoln
7. President of the Confederacy
8. Lincoln's vice president who became president when Lincoln died
9. Man who debated Abraham Lincoln for the Senate seat from Illinois
10. Man made commander of the Union armies by Lincoln after the first Battle of Bull Run
11. Robert E. Lee's best general
12. Nickname given to Thomas Jackson at the first Battle of Bull Run

## SITES OF WARFARE

1. Site of Southern surrender, ending the Civil War
2. Railroad center in Georgia that was destroyed by Sherman's troops
3. Town where Lincoln gave a famous speech at the dedication of a cemetery
4. River the North needed to control to split the South
5. Body of water into which the Mississippi empties
6. River on which Vicksburg is located
7. Body of water on which Savannah is a port
8. Site of the first major battle of the Civil War
9. Maryland city where Lee's troops were stopped during the Southern invasion of the North in 1862
10. First capital of the Confederacy
11. Battle that stopped the Confederate invasion of Pennsylvania
12. Major city on the Mississippi River that was captured in July 1863

## FACTORS RELATED TO THE WAR

1. Political party that Lincoln represented when he ran for the presidency
2. Major crop of the Southern states
3. Executive order that freed the slaves in rebel territory
4. This section of the country had greater industrial strength
5. Part of Virginia that did not leave the Union
6. The South's economy was based on this
7. Lincoln's occupation before he became president
8. Constitutional amendment that freed the slaves

## TERMS OF THE WAR

1. Withdrawal of a state from the Union
2. What Maryland, Kentucky, Missouri, and Delaware were called during the Civil War
3. Closing of Southern ports so that supplies could not be shipped in or out
4. Process of restoring normal relations between the states following the Civil War
5. To give up in a battle or war
6. In a war, the strategy of fighting to protect something or prevent being captured
7. In a war, the strategy of fighting to capture something
8. Organized groups of soldiers

5

10

©1978, 1988, 1997, 2002 Walch Publishing

9. People who have been killed or wounded in battle

10. Another name for fighting aims

11. Union plan for strangling the South

12. Long period of warfare in which Vicksburg was surrounded and starved into surrender

13. A long-range plan for winning a battle or war

14. Murder of a public official

15. Exploding underwater bombs

16. Ships with metal plates on their sides

---

9. Fast ships that dodged Union warships

10. Number of Confederate states

11. School that many great army officers attended

12. Northern ironclad ship

13. Southern ironclad that fought the *Monitor*

14. Famous speech that began, "Four score and seven years ago . . ."

15. One of the two European nations the Confederates thought would aid them in the war

16. This was one of the South's greatest military strengths

17. Army that General Lee commanded

---

13. Three Southern states that were cut off after the North gained control of the Mississippi

14. Important railroad center in southern Tennessee that was captured in September 1863

15. Area that refused to secede with Virginia and eventually became a separate state

16. River on which Washington, D.C., is located

17. City whose capture Sherman presented to Lincoln as a Christmas present

18. Battle in which Stonewall Jackson was shot

19. Four slaveholding border states

20. Site of battle of the ironclads

21. Creek along which Manassas Junction was located

---

13. Northern general most responsible for taking the Mississippi River

14. Northern general who made the March to the Sea

15. Man who designed the U.S.S. *Monitor*

16. Man who led the cavalry forces of the Confederacy until Yellow Tavern

17. Southern general who led a charge at the center of the Union line at Gettysburg

18. Northern admiral who captured New Orleans

19. Man who ran for the presidency against Lincoln in 1864

20. Lincoln's secretary of war whom Andrew Johnson tried to remove from office

21. Secretary of state in Lincoln's Cabinet

22. Leader of the Union army at Gettysburg

**15**

**20**

NOTES

# Reconstruction

| PEOPLE IN RECONSTRUCTION | RECONSTRUCTION IN PROGRESS | IMPORTANT LOCATIONS | TERMS OF RECONSTRUCTION |
|---|---|---|---|

**PEOPLE IN RECONSTRUCTION**

1. Northern politicians who went to the South after the Civil War
2. Man who shot Abraham Lincoln
3. Former slaves
4. Lincoln's vice president
5. Southerners who had not taken part in the war and who tried to help the North during Reconstruction
6. People who farmed another person's land, receiving a share of what they produced
7. Civil War general who became president after Andrew Johnson
8. High federal official impeached by the House of Representatives in 1867

**RECONSTRUCTION IN PROGRESS**

1. Procedure that President Johnson used in an effort to prevent the passage of many bills
2. Two rights denied many Southern males after the Civil War
3. What the members of the Ku Klux Klan dressed to resemble
4. One of the most important needs of the freed slaves, provided to hundreds of thousands of them during Reconstruction
5. Lawmaking body that felt it should handle the reconstruction of the states
6. A way of voting without anyone knowing how one has voted
7. Constitutional amendment that abolished slavery
8. Constitutional Amendment to which the Southern states had to agree before reentering the Union
9. Period of rebuilding after the Civil War
10. New federal agency established to help Southern blacks adjust to freedom
11. New laws passed by Southern states to keep blacks from voting

**IMPORTANT LOCATIONS**

1. City in which Lincoln was shot
2. Section of the country that suffered the most destruction and loss of life during the Civil War
3. First Southern state readmitted to the Union
4. Theater in which President Lincoln was shot
5. President Johnson's home state

**TERMS OF RECONSTRUCTION**

1. Tactic that the Ku Klux Klan used to get what it wanted from blacks
2. Status sought for African Americans by the Fourteenth and Fifteenth Amendments
3. State lawmaking bodies
4. To approve of an amendment or law by voting
5. Claim by whites that they were better than blacks
6. Social habits of a people
7. Removal of an officeholder before his or her term expires

5

10

*American History Challenge!*

©1978, 1988, 1997, 2002 Walch Publishing

8. Separation of the races

9. This described freed slaves who could not read or write.

10. During Reconstruction, this element controlled the South.

---

11. Rights of a citizen

12. Law that violates the Constitution

13. Favoring extreme changes

14. People who did not have full rights of citizenship

---

6. Five sections into which the Southern states that had not reentered the Union were divided

7. City and state in which Lincoln was buried

---

8. Nickname given to the Southern states after they began voting consistently for the Democratic party

9. Under state constitutions, a person no longer could be put here because of a debt

---

12. Constitutional amendment that made African Americans citizens

13. Constitutional amendment that gave black males the right to vote

14. Terrorist organization formed to oppress blacks

15. Political party to which most Southerners belonged after the Civil War

16. Law that President Johnson was accused of breaking

17. Lincoln's plan that would make it easy for the Southern states to be readmitted to the Union

---

18. Constitutional amendment that barred former office-holders who had fought against the Union from holding public office again

19. Month and year in which Lincoln was shot

20. Tax placed upon each person who registered to vote

21. Test to make sure people could read or write before they could vote

22. Nickname for laws that required segregation

---

9. Woman who helped create the American Red Cross

10. Group of Republicans who felt the South should be punished for the Civil War

11. Secretary of war in Lincoln's Cabinet

12. A farmer who owned animals and tools but farmed someone else's farm

**15**

---

13. Man who ran against Rutherford B. Hayes and almost became president

14. Person who presides at an impeachment trial

15. Senator from Massachusetts who agreed to help challenge Johnson's presidency

16. House of Representatives member who led the attack on Johnson

17. President who removed all federal troops from the South

**20**

---

NOTES

# Life on the Great Plains

## PEOPLE OF THE PLAINS

1. Early explorers sent out by President Jefferson to map the Great Plains

2. These fast riders carried letters between California and Missouri

3. Men who moved cattle from place to place

4. Native Americans who lived in the area of Kansas and Nebraska

5. Army commander killed at Little Bighorn

6. Largest and most powerful tribe of the Plains Indians

7. Leader, but not chief, of the Native Americans at Little Bighorn

## PLACES ON THE PLAINS

1. Eastern boundary of the Great Plains

2. Western boundary of the Great Plains

3. The Union Pacific and Central Pacific railroads met here to form the transcontinental railroad

4. Mountainous area shared by South Dakota and Wyoming

5. Most important river on the Great Plains

6. Famous fort in eastern Wyoming

## RANCHING AND SETTLEMENT

1. Natural vegetation of the Great Plains

2. Nickname for the Great Plains

3. Animal brought to the Great Plains by the early Spanish explorers

4. A mark burned into a cow's hide to show ownership

5. Cheap fencing for the Great Plains

6. When cattle run away, out of control

7. Period of time that homesteaders had to live on the land before it belonged to them

8. Kind of cattle first brought to the Great Plains

9. First railroad to cross the Great Plains

10. Unfenced grazing land

11. Form of transportation used by western cattlemen to ship cattle to eastern towns

## INDIAN LIFE

1. Animal that supplied the Plains Indians with most of their needs

2. What the Native Americans did not believe people could own

3. Occupation that government agents wanted Native Americans to take up

4. People who travel from place to place, as most Plains Indians did

5. Touching of an enemy by a warrior instead of killing him

6. Native American name for the railroad

7. An area of land set aside for the Native Americans' use

**5**

**10**

©1978, 1988, 1997, 2002 Walch Publishing

8. Food of shredded, dried meat mixed with fat eaten by the Native Americans
9. Nickname for the Battle of Little Bighorn
10. Conveyance that carried the Native Americans' belongings, pulled by a horse or a dog
11. Language used by people of different tribes to talk with one another

12. Fight between the settlers and the Sioux between 1876 and 1877
13. Infamous Native American massacre in Colorado
14. Name for the long, bitter journey taken by the Cherokee Indians after they were forced to give up their land in the East
15. Government agency in charge of matters involving the Native Americans

12. Vehicle that carried food on cattle drives
13. Material from which early homes were built on the Great Plains
14. Famous cattle trail that led from San Antonio, Texas, to Abilene, Kansas
15. Moving cattle from one place to another
16. Act passed by Congress, allowing farmers to get free land
17. What the government gave railroads large amounts of, to encourage railroad building in the West

18. Mechanism used on the Great Plains to bring water out of deep wells
19. Last of the Great Plains states to enter the union
20. Act passed in 1854 that allowed settlement of the Great Plains
21. These insects often came in such large numbers that they ate all the farmers' crops.

7. This place, which is now a state, was originally set aside for the Native Americans.
8. The Battle of Little Bighorn took place here.
9. Area in South Dakota reserved by the government for the Sioux until gold was discovered

10. Body of water into which the rivers of the Great Plains flow
11. Large pens where cattle were put before shipment to the East
12. Most western cattle were shipped on the railroad to this city.

8. Sioux chief, leader of Native American forces at Little Bighorn
9. The Apache Indians were led by this man.
10. Inventor of barbed wire
11. Commander of the military forces in Colorado at Sand Creek

12. Native American chief of the Cheyenne tribe at Sand Creek
13. People who qualified for free government lands
14. These Native Americans lived on the Columbia Plateau in Oregon.

15

20

NOTES

# New Inventions and Transportation

## BUILDERS AND DOERS

1. Immigrant who started one of America's largest steel companies
2. Man who started the Standard Oil Company
3. Inventor of the electric light
4. Man given credit for making the automobile cheap enough for Americans to buy
5. People who go to another country to live
6. Inventor of the telephone
7. Man who developed a camera that used rolls of film instead of plates
8. Immigrants to California during the Gold Rush who helped build the transcontinental railroad
9. Englishman who came up with a way to get the impurities out of iron by blowing air through it
10. Inventor of the sleeping car on trains
11. Inventor of interchangeable parts, an idea that Henry Ford borrowed
12. Man nicknamed "Lucky Lindy"

## IMPORTANT LOCATIONS

1. Cities along a coastline
2. Site of Carnegie's company and America's steel center
3. Where people went to live to be close to their jobs
4. State in which oil was first drilled near the town of Titusville
5. City where Henry Ford's factories were located, which became the center of the automobile industry
6. City where Lindbergh landed when he flew across the Atlantic
7. Site of the Wright brothers' airplane flight
8. City in which the Wright brothers' bicycle-repair shop was located
9. Cloth-making establishments that spread through the South after the Civil War
10. City near which the Central Pacific and Union Pacific railroads met to form the first transcontinental railroad

## INVENTIONS AND DISCOVERIES

1. Henry Ford's mass-produced low-priced car
2. Nickname for the early radio
3. Lindbergh's airplane
4. Invention that allowed farmers to fence cattle
5. Metal that replaced iron as a material for rails, enabling trains to carry heavier loads
6. Nickname for early automobiles
7. The new way steel was made from iron
8. Samuel F.B. Morse used this to send messages along wires.

## TERMS OF PROGRESS

1. Pieces that are exactly alike and can be used interchangeably in many products
2. Henry Ford's idea of moving the product past workers who then add parts to it
3. Another name for crude oil
4. Complete control of a product or service
5. Another name for trade
6. Procedure in which the work on a product is divided up and handled by people who become specialists
7. Great growth in technology when factories and machines replaced craft shops and hand tools
8. This was the best fuel to use in making steel.

**5**

**10**

©1978, 1988, 1997, 2002 Walch Publishing

9. To use money with the hope of making a profit

10. Making or producing things on a large scale

11. Application of science to machinery and new methods of industrial production

12. Use of machines and mechanical systems that operate with little or no human control

13. Making a small down payment on a product and then small regular payments later

14. Factors of production

15. Number of stores under the same management located in various cities

16. Crowded, rundown apartment houses in cities

9. Invention that Marconi helped perfect

10. Device that allows air to be forced through melted iron, removing impurities from the iron

11. Ore from which aluminum is obtained

12. Machine that changes waterpower or steam into electricity

13. Office machine invented in 1867, once used widely by writers and businesses

14. Nickname for the Model T

11. Places in which modern workers worked instead of at home

12. Country from which Andrew Carnegie came as a young man

13. City in which Edison's workshop was located

14. State in which the first telephone service was established

15. City in which KDKA, the first radio station, was located

16. Our nation's greatest iron ore deposits were found near this Great Lake.

17. Small factories that have poor working conditions

18. Jane Addams started this as a community center to help immigrants.

13. Man who assisted in the invention of the telephone

14. Inventor of the air brake for trains

15. Man responsible for laying second and much improved telegraph cable under the Atlantic Ocean

16. Man who made the first solo, nonstop flight from New York to Paris in 1927

17. The telegraph was invented by this man.

18. First man to fly in an airplane

19. Man who perfected the elevator

20. Man who started the first five-and-ten-cent store

21. The reaper or crop harvester was invented by this man.

22. A person who works to bring about change for the better

23. Woman who worked to educate and train immigrants

15

20

NOTES

©1978, 1988, 1997, 2002 Walch Publishing

# America Becomes a World Power

## IMPORTANT LEADERS

1. English explorer who reached the Hawaiian Islands in 1778
2. Leader of the Rough Riders during America's war with Spain
3. President of the United States when the Panama Canal was opened
4. Man who urged Congress to purchase Alaska
5. President who blocked an attempt to make Hawaii a possession of the United States
6. Man who said the United States should "speak softly and carry a big stick"
7. President when Hawaii was annexed
8. U.S. admiral at Manila Bay
9. President when the Panama Canal was begun
10. Army doctor appointed to govern Cuba after the Spanish-American war
11. Cuban doctor who believed that yellow fever was carried by mosquitoes
12. Man who helped stamp out yellow fever in Panama before building the canal
13. Secretary of state who opened trade with China

## PLACES AMERICAN POWER SPREAD

1. Area of land purchased by the United States in 1867
2. Area called Seward's Folly
3. Famous harbor in the Hawaiian Islands
4. Country through which the United States built a canal
5. Fiftieth state
6. Country that sold the Virgin Islands to the United States
7. Bodies of water connected by the Panama Canal
8. Body of water that lies north of Alaska
9. Harbor in which the *Maine* was blown up
10. Islands bought by the United States to protect the Panama Canal
11. Nation that sold Alaska to the United States
12. Country that controlled Puerto Rico before 1898
13. Narrow body of water that separates Asia from North America
14. Bay on which Manila is a seaport
15. Location of Manila
16. Place charged by the Rough Riders
17. Area of Russia close to Alaska

## ITEMS AND EVENTS

1. Battleship sent to protect Americans living in Havana
2. Insect that army doctors found carried yellow fever
3. Mechanisms built into the Panama Canal to raise and lower water levels so ships could pass through
4. Religious people who hoped to convert Hawaiians to the Christian faith
5. Metal whose discovery made many people rush to Alaska
6. Two diseases that killed many Americans in Cuba
7. Product of the Hawaiian Islands desired by Americans

## TERMS OF POWER

1. Feeling of pride in your country
2. Harsh and unjust rule
3. This formal agreement usually follows an armistice or a cease-fire.
4. Freedom from control by others
5. Small groups of fighters who strike suddenly without warning and then disappear
6. Process by which the United States took over Hawaii
7. People who wanted the United States to gain new territories
8. Policy of extending the rule of an empire or a nation over foreign countries

**5**

**10**

9. Idea that every nation would have equal trading rights with China

10. An agreement to stop fighting

11. A large, sudden change in government and peoples' lives

12. A change for the better

---

13. Information or ideas that are spread to help or hurt a cause, group, or nation

14. Practice of featuring sensational news with large headlines to sell papers

15. Theodore Roosevelt's quote indicating the United States would try to achieve its aims quietly, keeping warfare as an option

16. Theodore Roosevelt and his supporters were called this.

17. To have the government set rules for business, transportation, and banking

---

8. Ship whose destruction caused the United States to declare war on Spain

9. Original inhabitants of the Hawaiian Islands

10. Battleship whose late arrival in Cuba during the Spanish-American War showed the need for a Central American canal

---

11. Cuban crop in which many Americans invested

12. Act that made the people of Puerto Rico citizens of the United States

13. War that lasted only 100 days

14. Theodore Roosevelt became the first American to receive this.

---

18. Country in which many Americans felt a canal should be built rather than in Panama

19. Country in which the Boxer Rebellion occurred

20. Forty-ninth state

21. Term meaning eastern Asia

22. American naval base established on Cuba to help protect the Canal

23. Sea in which Cuba is situated

24. Group of islands in which early U.S. possessions in the Pacific were located

---

25. Site of the U.S. naval base on the Samoan Islands

26. Nation that controlled the Philippine Islands before 1898

27. Country that controlled Panama before the United States helped the area rebel

28. Two islands in the Pacific Ocean that the United States took in 1898

29. Three territories gained by the United States from Spain at the end of the Spanish-American War

---

14. Commander of U.S. fleet that opened Japan to U.S. trade

15. Man who gave America its claim to the Hawaiian Islands

16. Man who set up pineapple plantations in Hawaii

17. Man whose newspapers helped get the United States into the Spanish-American War

18. Lincoln's secretary of state

19. First white man to visit the area of Alaska

---

20. Last Hawaiian monarch

21. Filipino leader who wanted his nation to become independent in 1898

22. American doctor who headed the Yellow Fever Commission, which discovered the cause of yellow fever

23. Chief engineer of the Panama Canal

24. President of the United States when it purchased the Virgin Islands

25. This king united the Hawaiian Islands.

---

15

20

NOTES

# 21 Government, Business, and Labor

## IMPORTANT LEADERS

1. Man who established the Standard Oil Trust
2. First president of the A.F.L. (American Federation of Labor)
3. Man who made a fortune in steel
4. Man who helped form the C.I.O. (Congress of Industrial Organizations)
5. President known as the Trustbuster because he fought the trusts
6. President who was shot while attending the Pan-American Exposition in 1901
7. Leader of the United Mine Workers
8. Man who established the Grange in 1867

## GETTING ORGANIZED

1. First national labor organization
2. Organizations of workers formed to get higher pay and better working conditions
3. Refusal by union workers to work
4. Written agreement that lists working conditions and wages
5. Labor organization that replaced the Knights of Labor
6. Another name for a railroad union
7. Kind of union made up of workers in a single trade
8. Procedure in which workers' representatives discuss wages and working conditions with management
9. Nonunion workers who cross union picket lines to work
10. Organization established by farmers to work for their interests
11. Kind of union not limited to workers of a single trade

## FORMS OF BUSINESS

1. Situation in which one business without competition controls a service or product
2. Amount of money received after expenses are paid
3. Effort of a business firm to try to win customers from other firms
4. Joining of several people to start a company
5. People who work in a business
6. Consumer wants and needs are called this.
7. Procedure in which two railroads serving the same area agreed to charge all shippers the same rate
8. Shipment of products made in one state to dealers and customers in other states
9. Shares of the profits of a company that are distributed among stockholders
10. What people receive when they invest in a corporation
11. Money returned to big businesses by the railroads
12. People who own a corporation

## REGULATION BY LAW

1. Merit system established in 1883 that covered government office workers
2. Correct name of the Wagner Act, which allowed workers to join unions of their choice
3. Act passed to protect the nation's health
4. Act passed in 1890 to do away with company mergers that restrained competition
5. Law passed in 1887 to control trade between the states
6. Body established by the Interstate Commerce Act to supervise the business of all railroads

5

10

©1978, 1988, 1997, 2002 Walch Publishing

7. Act that set up agricultural schools and colleges in many states

8. Law that established the 40-hour workweek and the minimum wage

9. Strong law passed in 1914 to control trusts

10. Law passed to guarantee workers the right to organize

11. Act passed after World War II to control labor unions

12. Fire in which 146 garment workers died, prompting the passage of laws to improve working conditions

13. People who start their own companies

14. Business owned by many people who own stock in that business

15. Group of people who run a corporation

16. Money and equipment needed to run a business

17. Several large businesses joined together to do away with competition

18. Joining of one business with another

19. Huge modern company that controls many businesses in different fields

20. Type of company created to gain controlling interest in other companies

21. Term that means a stockholder cannot be held personally responsible for the debts of a corporation

22. A system in which businesses have the freedom to sell many kinds of goods and services and people have the freedom to buy what they want or need

12. Postponement of a strike for a specific number of days ordered by the president

13. Withholding of employment and closing of businesses by employers during a strike

14. Court orders forbidding workers to strike or to picket

15. City where the Pullman Strike occurred in 1894

16. Agreement between a union and a company that only union members would be hired

17. Contract that workers had to sign stating they were not and would not become union members

18. Protest meeting in Chicago that erupted into violence unfairly blamed on the Knights of Labor

19. Oldest union that still exists today

20. "Wobblies"

9. Man who gained control of a railroad empire

10. Man who became president after McKinley was shot

11. Man who followed Theodore Roosevelt as president

12. Man who built up one of the world's leading banking houses

13. Man who organized the Knights of Labor

14. Man who destroyed the Knights of Labor by calling too many strikes

15. Two men who sponsored the Labor-Management Relations Act of 1947

16. Leader of the American Railway Union in 1894

17. Author of *The Jungle*, a book that exposed conditions in the meat-packing industry

15

20

NOTES

# World War I

| IMPORTANT PEOPLE | SITES OF WAR | WAR WORDS AND PHRASES | WAR ON THE WATER |
|---|---|---|---|

**WAR ON THE WATER**

1. Strait between England and France
2. Strait that controls the entrance to the Mediterranean Sea
3. Body of water where most of the unrestricted submarine warfare occurred
4. German vessels that sank many Allied ships
5. Body of water into which the Adriatic Sea flows
6. Means by which the British were able to bottle up the German navy at home
7. Artificial waterway that connects the Mediterranean and Red seas
8. Sea that is the site of Russia's only warm-weather port
9. Strait between Spain and Africa
10. Body of water that lies between England and Norway
11. Body of water connected by the Suez Canal to the Mediterranean Sea
12. Site of Russia's "window to the sea"

**WAR WORDS AND PHRASES**

1. Protective ditches dug by soldiers
2. Armored combat vehicles first used during World War 1
3. Hand-thrown bombs
4. Policy of one nation owning or controlling another
5. The peace treaty ending World War I was called this.
6. Alliance formed by Germany, Italy, and Austria-Hungary
7. Alliance formed by England, France, and Russia
8. Term for Germany, Austria-Hungary, Bulgaria, and Turkey
9. Idea that decisions should be based only on what is good for your own country
10. Wilson's plan for peace
11. Another name for a cease-fire agreement
12. New invention used mainly for scouting enemy troop movements
13. Calling up of men to serve in the army
14. Term for England, France, Russia, and the United States

**SITES OF WAR**

1. Nation called the Dual Monarchy
2. Palace where the treaty ending World War I was signed
3. Country invaded by Germany on its way to attack France
4. Country where Archduke Ferdinand was assassinated
5. Nation that withdrew from the Triple Alliance
6. Battle line in France
7. Nation with the world's strongest navy before the war
8. Battle line in Russia
9. Country that entered the war when Belgium was invaded
10. Country that withdrew from the war because of an internal revolution
11. Nation whose neutrality was broken, causing Great Britain to enter the war
12. Major neutral nation at the start of the war

**IMPORTANT PEOPLE**

1. Man whose assassination started World War I
2. Head of the German government during the war
3. President of the United States during the war
4. Head of the American armed forces
5. This man asked Congress to declare war on Germany.
6. He said, "The world must be made safe for democracy."
7. British representative at the Versailles Peace Conference
8. French representative at the Versailles Peace Conference
9. Man who proposed the Fourteen Points
10. German foreign minister who sent a note to the Mexicans attempting to persuade them to invade the United States
11. The Red Baron
12. Overall commander of the Allied armies

**5**

**10**

©1978, 1988, 1997, 2002 Walch Publishing

13. Two straits that Russia wanted to control to have access to the Mediterranean

14. River on which Paris is located

15. Body of water on which Russia's port of Murmansk is located

16. Body of water on which the British fleet was stationed

17. Body of water that borders Yugoslavia

18. Site of Germany's only port

19. Germany's all-out submarine attacks

20. System that the Allies developed to defend against submarine attacks

21. First Allied passenger liner to be sunk with a loss of American lives

22. French passenger ship that was sunk, prompting the second protest by the United States to Germany

23. Place where the German navy was defeated by the British

15. Term for an American soldier in the war

16. Competition between nations for the highest number of weapons of war

17. Another name for the American army during the war

18. This was the land between armies in trench warfare.

19. Germany's description of the Belgian neutrality treaty

20. Position taken by the United States during the early years of the war

21. Policy by which a nation retreats from involvement with the world

22. Situation that exists when all nations have equal power

23. Policy by which a nation is free to determine its own political status

24. World's first international political organization

25. Planned effort to shape people's ideas and opinions

26. Germany, at the end of the war, agreed to make these to pay for damages done in the war.

13. Nation with the best army in Europe before the war

14. Largest nation to fight in the war

15. Peninsula that both Germany and Russia wanted to control

16. Country that agreed to aid Austria-Hungary after the assassination

17. Nation from which Latvia, Estonia, and Lithuania were formed after the war

18. Nation carved out of Austria-Hungary after the war

19. Country that received the major blame for the war

20. Country on the other side of the Western Front from Germany

21. This battle was the turning point of World War I.

22. In September 1918, the first major American offensive occurred here.

23. Forest on the Meuse River in which Americans fought

13. Tsar of Russia during the war

14. Man who said World War I should be "the war to end all wars"

15. Italian representative at the Versailles Peace Conference

16. German leader who unified his nation before the war

17. Man sent by Wilson to Europe to arrange an early peace

18. Tsar who took charge of the Russian forces early in the war

19. Planner of the German attack on Paris through Belgium

20. Mexican revolutionary who led Pershing on a chase before the war

21. Assassin of Archduke Ferdinand

22. America's flying ace

15

20

N O T E S

# Between the World Wars

## IMPORTANT PEOPLE

1. Man elected president in 1920

2. "Silent Cal"

3. President of the United States at the start of the Great Depression

4. President remembered for the scandals that occurred during his administration

5. Man who promised a "new deal" in government if he were elected

6. Man who became president when Harding died

7. Man who led the fight in the United States against acceptance of the League of Nations

8. Secretary of state who arranged a pact with Aristide Briand to outlaw war

## DOMESTIC BOOM AND BUST

1. Act that set up retirement funds and unemployment insurance

2. Franklin Delano Roosevelt's plan for recovery from the Depression

3. New Deal project that employed young men to help plant forests

4. Political party to which Harding, Coolidge, and Hoover all belonged

5. Term meaning people without jobs

6. Nickname for the period of high times in the United States following World War I

7. Constitutional amendment that outlawed the sale of alcoholic beverages in the United States

8. Period of extreme economic collapse

9. Market in which many people had invested that collapsed in October 1929

10. Constitutional amendment that gave women the right to vote

## SITES OF ACTION

1. Oil reserve in Wyoming that was part of the Harding scandal

2. City in which the arms conference that followed World War I was held

3. This is a site where people can buy and sell securities.

4. Three major nations that attended the arms conference following World War I

5. California oil reserve that was part of the Harding scandals

6. River on which massive dams were built to control flooding and provide more electric power

## INTERNATIONAL EVENTS

1. First attempt at a world peace organization

2. World peace organization the United States did not join

3. House of Congress that had to ratify the Versailles treaty

4. Organization set up to use international law to settle disputes between nations

5. Conference of world nations that met to reduce the size of their navies after World War I

6. Americans who did not want the United States to be involved with Europe anymore

5

10

©1978, 1988, 1997, 2002 Walch Publishing

7. Woodrow Wilson's phrase describing the effects of World War I on the world

8. System that determined how many immigrants the United States would accept each year from each country

9. Organization set up by the League of Nations to deal with the problems of workers everywhere

10. Agreement that in 1928 outlawed war as a means of settling problems

7. A period of drought made farming in this area almost impossible.

8. Nation whose people were angered by the new immigration system

9. Sites where homeless unemployed people camped together during the Depression

10. Site of world conference called by the League of Nations to discuss limiting arms

11. The League of Nations set up headquarters here.

12. The World Court was located here.

11. A period of time in which there is little money and no economic growth

12. Business for which President Franklin Roosevelt declared a "holiday" to see if they were sound enough to reopen

13. New Deal program that hired people to work on public projects such as highways and buildings

14. New Deal project that built dams to control flooding and increase electrical power

15. New Deal project whose initials were WPA

16. New Deal project that gave aid to farmers

17. Roosevelt's radio talks to the nation

18. A body of government officials and employees

9. President who died of illness in office

10. Man who said, "The only thing we have to fear is fear itself."

11. This man was elected president of the United States even though he had polio.

12. American lawyer who was chairman of the committee that drew up plans for the World Court

13. U.S. secretary of state who opened the Washington Conference on naval arms limitations

14. Secretary of the interior involved in the oil scandals

15. This woman, who was Teddy Roosevelt's niece, married Franklin Roosevelt.

15

20

NOTES

# 24

# Economics

## IMPORTANT PEOPLE

1. Person who studies how things are bought, sold, and used by a society
2. People who hire others to work for them
3. Person who owns stock in a corporation
4. Person who exchanges one item for another
5. People who work in a business
6. A person who owes money
7. Person who becomes expert in one kind of work
8. Person who puts money into a venture in the hope of earning more money
9. Person who uses goods and services

**5**

**10**

## PLACES IN OUR ECONOMY

1. Building or group of buildings in which goods are made
2. Places where money is kept, loaned, and exchanged
3. A small factory that has poor working conditions
4. System in which a product is sent from one worker to another for parts
5. Home of the New York Stock Exchange

## THINGS IN THE U.S. ECONOMY

1. Products that humans need or want
2. Money earned for work done
3. Money that is borrowed
4. Anything that is accepted as a medium of exchange
5. Money left over after a company's expenses have been paid
6. Money paid by people for the support of their government
7. Amount for which a thing can be bought or sold
8. An item put in a newspaper or magazine to attract buyers
9. Security given to a bank in order to get a loan
10. Amount owed on a loan
11. Jobs people perform in return for payment
12. Money or property that a person or company uses in carrying on a business
13. Money paid by people for the use of bank money over a period of time
14. Place where a seller and a buyer meet to exchange goods

## ECONOMIC PRINCIPLES

1. Dividing up of the work to be done
2. Exchange of one item for another
3. To return a used item for further use
4. To refuse to buy something in order to show disapproval
5. Economic term for the situation that exists when money is less valuable and prices go up
6. Manufacture of something in quantity, usually by machines
7. Too small a supply of goods and services to meet demands
8. Economic system based on private ownership of goods and the means of producing them in a free market
9. Use of money to buy some form of property or goods from which a person expects to make a profit
10. Things people like to have but that are not essential to life
11. Period of good times and low unemployment

©1978, 1988, 1997, 2002 Walch Publishing

12. Amount of something available for sale
13. Division of the workday into three periods of eight hours each
14. Reliance of two or more people on one another for help, support, or an exchange of goods
15. Slowing of business activity that is not as severe as a depression
16. Drop in prices that occurs when the demand for goods is less than the supply
17. Spending by a government in excess of the amount it collects in taxes

18. Economic system in which private citizens own and control business and economic resources
19. Study to find out what people are likely to buy
20. Period of economic hard times, when prices are down and money is hard to get
21. Desire and ability to buy something
22. When a buyer pays only a small part of the price of an item and then makes regular payments until the debt is paid

15. Money paid to the government on a worker's wages
16. Written promise to repay at a given time, with interest, money borrowed by a corporation or the government
17. Written order to a bank to pay someone a sum of money
18. Money paid to stockholders out of company profits
19. Money that remains after taxes and other things have been taken out of the gross income

20. Money or something else that is accepted by the people of a culture for goods and services
21. Large businesses that are owned by stockholders
22. Plan that shows how money will be spent
23. Goods and services that fill human wants and needs
24. Total goods and services produced by a country during a year
25. The amount of money it takes to run a business

6. Center in New York where stocks and bonds are bought and sold
7. A factory that changes oil into fuels such as gasoline

8. Organizations whose members buy and sell securities for the public and for themselves
9. Place where goods are sold to consumers
10. Place where retail merchants can buy goods for their stores

10. Person who buys and sells stocks and bonds for others
11. A person who makes goods or supplies a service
12. A person who owns a business or shop
13. A person to whom money is owed

14. Merchant who buys goods in large amounts and sells them to retail stores
15. Person who brings together economic factors such as land, labor, and capital in order to make a profit
16. Person who buys goods to sell to individual consumers
17. People in charge of a business or an industry

15

20

NOTES

# 25

# America at Home, 1920–1940

| LAW AND CRIME | ENTERTAINMENT | SLANG COMES OF AGE | THE SPORTS WORLD |
|---|---|---|---|

**THE SPORTS WORLD**

1. Famous New York Yankee home-run hitter
2. Boxer called the Manassa Mauler
3. Young spelunker who became stuck in a cave in Kentucky and died there 18 days later
4. Museum established in 1936 at Cooperstown, New York, to honor baseball players
5. Stadium known as the House That Ruth Built
6. Boxer who knocked out Jack Dempsey in the famous "long count"
7. Famous American Indian who won the Olympic pentathlon and decathlon medals but had to return them
8. Racehorse, also called Big Red, who won 20 out of 21 starts

**SLANG COMES OF AGE**

1. Flapper
2. Big cheese
3. Blind date
4. Bump off
5. Crush
6. Hoofer
7. Jalopy
8. Upchuck
9. G-men
10. Hard-boiled
11. Gold digger
12. Fall guy

**ENTERTAINMENT**

1. Movie that introduced talkies
2. Famous black trumpet player who got his start in the twenties
3. Country's first radio station (in Pittsburgh)
4. Famous humorist and actor who said, "All I know is what I read in the papers."
5. Word puzzles that first appeared in the 1920s
6. Famous movie of 1939 that takes place during the Civil War
7. Feat for which Shipwreck Kelly became known
8. Author of *Main Street* and *Babbitt*
9. Famous novel by John Steinbeck about the movement of workers from Oklahoma to California
10. Four famous brothers who made many comedy movies
11. Actor who played in *The Sheik* and was a Hollywood idol
12. Composer of *Rhapsody in Blue*
13. Famous dance of the 1920s that took its name from a city

**LAW AND CRIME**

1. Famous Chicago gangster who was eventually arrested for income tax evasion
2. Constitutional amendment that prohibited buying and selling of liquor, causing many people to break the law
3. Two immigrants who were arrested, tried, and executed for a robbery and murder in South Braintree, Massachusetts
4. Famous trial over the question of evolution held in Dayton, Tennessee
5. Agency whose members arrested or killed many gangsters in the 1930s
6. Flyer whose son was kidnapped and murdered, shocking the nation
7. People who transported and sold illegal liquor
8. Small metal container for carrying illegal liquor

**5**

**10**

©1978, 1988, 1997, 2002 Walch Publishing

9. Man who played for the Detroit Tigers and led the American League in batting for 12 years

10. Man who dominated world tennis from 1920 to 1927

11. Winner of the grand slam in golf in 1930

12. First American woman to swim the English Channel

13. Great Olympic swimmer who went on to play Tarzan in the movies

14. Notre Dame football coach whose teams lost only 12 games from 1919 to 1931

15. Football great known as the Galloping Ghost

16. Great black athlete who dominated the 1936 Olympics

13. Cat's meow

14. Lousy

15. Pinch

16. Scram

17. Torpedo

18. Spiffy

19. The real McCoy

20. Gam

21. Berries

22. Bee's knees

23. Jazz

14. Famous comedian known for his baggy pants and little mustache

15. Nonstop dance competition

16. Radio program that was broadcast on Halloween night and caused panic

17. President Franklin Roosevelt's informal radio broadcasts to the nation

18. Renowned dance partner of Ginger Rogers

19. Child star known for her ringlets

20. Author of *The Great Gatsby*

21. Dance named for Irene and Vernon Castle

22. Actor who played in *The Hunchback of Notre Dame* and other horror films

23. Child star who played Andy Hardy in many movies

24. Man who wrote 20 plays during the 1920s and won the Pulitzer Prize for 3 of them

25. Reporter, editor, and author who wrote for the *American Mercury* and was known as the man who hated everything

26. This man was the first to fly solo across the Atlantic Ocean.

9. Nightclubs where illegal liquor was sold

10. Nickname for homemade liquor

11. Man who became head of the FBI

12. Attack in which Al Capone's gang entered a garage and machine-gunned members of the Moran gang

13. Two teenagers defended by Clarence Darrow for the murder of Bobby Franks

14. Most notorious bank robber

15. Famous bank robber known as Pretty Boy

16. Woman gangster known as Ma

15

20

NOTES

# 26

# The World Heads Toward War

## THE LEADERS

1. President of the United States at the start of World War II
2. Man who said, "I believe it is peace in our time."
3. Secretary of state who, with Aristide Briand, agreed to outlaw war
4. This man became dictator of Germany.
5. Man who came to power in 1922 and became Italy's dictator
6. Leader of the Soviet Union
7. Dictator of Spain
8. British prime minister at Munich
9. Secretary of state who issued the Stimson Doctrine

## THE PLACES

1. Country whose leader was Mussolini
2. Country ruled by Hitler
3. Territory invaded by Germany in 1936
4. Nation that was never a member of the League of Nations
5. City at which a conference was held to decide the fate of Czechoslovakia
6. Capital of Germany
7. Capital of Italy
8. Nation attacked by Japan in 1931
9. African nation attacked by Mussolini
10. Nation that withdrew from the agreements of the Washington Conference so it could increase its navy

## THINGS PEOPLE TALKED ABOUT

1. French-fortified line between Germany and France
2. Agreement that limited Germany's army
3. What most people felt would protect the United States
4. Name given to Mussolini
5. Hitler blamed all of Germany's problems on these people.
6. The German National Socialists were called this.
7. New name given to Manchuria
8. Objective of the Washington Conference of 1921–1922

## IDEAS THAT LED TO WAR

1. Hands-off policy of the United States in the 1930s
2. Ruler who has complete control of the government and the people of a nation
3. Not taking sides in a war
4. Agreements between nations to help in case of war
5. Government that has complete control over individuals
6. Pacifying or satisfying rather than going to war
7. People's loyalty and pride in their country

5

10

©1978, 1988, 1997, 2002 Walch Publishing

8. Money that Germany was to pay for damages caused in World War I

9. Use of military force to conquer the land of another nation

10. Term made up by Mussolini to refer to Germany and Italy

---

11. Opposition to war or violence as a method of settling disputes

12. A nation in which the commands of the dictator are law

13. A way to force people to serve in the military

---

9. Body established to check aggression

10. Period of economic collapse that helped cause World War II

11. Acts that isolationists got Congress to pass from 1935 to 1937

12. These German troops burned books and attacked Jewish people.

---

13. U.S. ship bombed and sunk by Japan in China on December 12, 1937

14. Act that prohibited the U.S. government from lending money to any country that had not paid its war debts from World War I

15. German-fortified line between France and Germany

16. Top-secret project that developed the first atomic bomb

17. Limiting what people could buy by issuing coupon books

---

11. Nation attacked by Japan in 1937

12. Country to which Franklin Roosevelt agreed to extend the protection of the Monroe Doctrine in 1938

13. Nation whose aggression prompted the Stimson Doctrine

14. This nation became communistic before World War II.

---

15. Country annexed by Germany in March 1938

16. Country in which a civil war occurred before World War II

17. Country in which Hitler was born

18. Only country to repay its debts from World War I

19. Section of Czechoslovakia that Hitler wanted

---

10. Emperor of Japan

11. This man was known as the Führer.

12. Secretary of state under Roosevelt

13. French premier at Munich

14. Leader of China

---

15. Emperor of Ethiopia

16. German immigrant who wrote to President Roosevelt about the possibility of developing the atomic bomb

17. Italian immigrant who helped build the first atomic reactor

18. This man went to the League of Nations for help when his country was attacked in 1935.

---

15

20

NOTES

# 27

# World War II

| CIVILIAN LEADERS | MILITARY LEADERS | WAR IN EUROPE AND AFRICA | WAR IN THE PACIFIC |
|---|---|---|---|

**WAR IN THE PACIFIC**

1. Nation that attacked the United States at Pearl Harbor
2. Country that occupied Indochina in July 1941
3. Body of water in which the Hawaiian Islands are located
4. Site at which the U.S. fleet was largely destroyed in 1941
5. Nation that U.S. planes supplied by flying "the Hump"
6. Islands that MacArthur had to leave to avoid being captured by the Japanese

7. Capital of the Philippines
8. City on which the first atomic bomb was dropped
9. Important air battles were fought by planes based on these ships.
10. The surrender of the Japanese occurred aboard this American battleship.
11. City on which the second atomic bomb was dropped
12. One of the Solomon Islands occupied by Japan in 1942

**WAR IN EUROPE AND AFRICA**

1. First nation to fall to the Blitzkrieg
2. Body of water over which part of the Battle of Britain occurred
3. Water passage in North Africa that the Germans wanted control of
4. Nation with which Germany signed a nonaggression pact early in 1939
5. Body of water on which all of Germany's ports were located
6. Body of water controlled by the Strait of Bosporus

7. Country attacked by the Soviet Union after the fall of Poland
8. Place where the Germans trapped the British and French forces
9. Nation that fell to Germany in June 1940
10. Capital of German-controlled France
11. Country to which the Lend-Lease Act was extended because of Hitler's attack in 1941
12. Nation that held power over Indochina before the war
13. Country invaded on D day

**MILITARY LEADERS**

1. Allied leader at Normandy on D day
2. According to the Constitution, this man was commander in chief during World War II.
3. Man who received the Japanese surrender on the battleship *Missouri*

4. Man who led the invasion of North Africa
5. American commander who left the Philippines
6. German leader in North Africa
7. This admiral was in charge of the invasion of Okinawa.

**CIVILIAN LEADERS**

1. Dictator of Germany during the war
2. Dictator of Italy during the war
3. Military leader of Japan during the war
4. British prime minister during most of the war
5. Leader of the Soviet Union during the war
6. Man who became president of the United States upon the death of Franklin Roosevelt

7. U.S. president during the Yalta Conference
8. This man asked Congress to declare war on December 8, 1941.
9. Man known as the Führer
10. U.S. president during the Potsdam Conference
11. Leader of the German-controlled French government
12. Many jobs in factories, fields, and offices were held by these people.

**5**

**10**

©1978, 1988, 1997, 2002 Walch Publishing

13. Two islands that became important as air bases in the American drive toward Japan

14. British naval base taken by Japan in 1942

15. Site of famous Death March

16. Islands the United States feared Japan would use to invade Alaska

17. U.S. fortress guarding Manila Bay

18. Site of the Battle of Leyte Gulf

19. Hawaiian island on which Pearl Harbor is located

20. Place where the U.S. Navy stopped the Japanese attack aimed at Australia

21. Body of water that lies northeast of Australia and west of the Solomon Islands

22. Body of water that lies between Japan and China

14. Battle that stopped the German advance in Egypt

15. Country in which Normandy is located

16. "Soft underbelly" of Europe

17. Country in which the Suez Canal is located

18. Conference at which Roosevelt and Churchill gave land in Asia to Russia

19. Country attacked by Italy in April 1939

20. Town where France signed its surrender in a railroad car

21. Place where the first meeting between Winston Churchill and Franklin Roosevelt occurred

22. Body of water crossed by Mussolini to invade Albania

23. The Allied invasion on D day occurred on these beaches.

24. With this device, British pilots could spot German planes at night.

25. Soviet troops stopped a German invasion at this city.

8. American leader of the Flying Tigers

9. German leader at Normandy on D day

10. British commander in North Africa

11. Two U.S. admirals of the Pacific fleet

12. German commander of the Luftwaffe

13. U.S. Army chief of staff

13. This German Jew came to the United States, where his theories helped produce the atomic bomb.

14. This woman was opposed to the way Japanese Americans were treated by their government.

15. King of England during World War II

16. Man who replaced Churchill as prime minister

17. Dictator killed by his own people

18. German minister of propaganda

19. Head of the German secret police

20. Man responsible for solving what Hitler called the Jewish problem

21. Leader of the Chinese Nationalist government during the war

22. Leader of the Free French government

23. Man who ran for president in 1944 against Franklin Roosevelt

15

20

NOTES

# The Postwar Years

**28**

## PEOPLE IN THE NEWS

1. U.S. president at the end of World War II
2. Man who sought Fair Deal legislation
3. Person who has served in the armed forces
4. Man who ran for the presidency in 1948 on the Republican ticket

5. First secretary general of the United Nations
6. Truman's secretary of state
7. Military man made secretary of state in 1947
8. This man was named Allied military commander of Japan after Japan surrendered.

## POSTWAR TERMS

1. Nickname used in World War II to refer to enlisted men
2. Labor work stoppage
3. Basic rights and freedoms of all people
4. A social and an economic system in which all land and industries are owned by the government

5. To discharge from military service
6. Substantial rise in prices and loss of buying power
7. Period of unarmed conflict between the United States and the Soviet Union after World War II
8. People made homeless by the war

## LAWS AND ORGANIZATIONS

1. Cabinet department created by the National Security Act
2. World organization established after World War II
3. Part of the United Nations that acts as police authority of the world
4. UN organization for which WHO stands

5. Part of the United Nations that handles translations and paperwork
6. Part of the United Nations in which all nations get one vote
7. Law passed to help veterans go to school and buy homes
8. Law passed in 1947 that required a 60-day waiting period before a contract could be ended

## PLACES IN THE NEWS

1. City where the Soviet Union stopped all inbound traffic in 1948
2. Country in which the United Nations is located
3. Nation divided among the United States, Great Britain, France, and the Soviet Union

4. Country in which the Yalta Conference took place
5. City in which Dumbarton Oaks is located
6. City divided into four occupation zones

**5**

**10**

©1978, 1988, 1997, 2002 Walch Publishing

7. The International Court of Justice, or World Court, meets here.

8. City where German war criminals were tried

9. Permanent members of the Security Council

10. Site of United Nations conference attended by 50 nations

---

11. Nation formed from the British, American, and French zones

12. Site of meeting to prepare a rough plan for a postwar United Nations

13. After World War II, the United States began to have trouble with this major nation.

---

9. The only political party in the Soviet Union

10. Agency of the United Nations that handles legal disputes among nations

11. Act that gave the government a monopoly on the production of fissionable materials

12. Part of the United Nations that studies the social, cultural, and health problems of nations

---

13. Constitutional amendment that limited a president's stay in office to two terms or eight years

14. Long-range plan to help Europe recover from the war

15. Group put in charge of the production and use of atomic energy in the United States

16. Government agency established after World War II that was located at the Massachusetts Institute of Technology

---

9. Have-not nations

10. Term meaning the person who heads the United Nations

11. Court order telling a union not to strike

12. Term for the 60-day waiting period before a contract could be ended

---

13. What many southern Democrats began calling themselves in the 1948 elections

14. Elements such as uranium that can be used to produce atomic energy

15. The policy that communism must not be allowed to expand into new countries

16. Term meaning to get vital supplies into an area by air

---

9. Second secretary general of the United Nations

10. Jewish girl killed in a concentration camp whose diary was found after World War II

11. People who the FBI and the Department of Justice began to investigate

12. President to whom the Twenty-second Amendment did not apply

---

13. Groups required by the McCarran Act to file their membership lists with the attorney general

14. Soviet ambassador at Dumbarton Oaks

15. Nazis tried at Nuremberg for torturing and murdering defenseless people

---

15

20

NOTES

# 29

# The Korean War

## WAR LEADERS

1. President of the United States during the Korean War

2. Chinese leader whom Douglas MacArthur wanted the United Nations to help

3. Russian premier who died in March 1953

4. Man who became president of the United States in January 1953

5. Man who became the commander of United Nations forces in Korea

6. Communist leader of China

7. President of South Korea

## SITES OF WARFARE

1. Country where war broke out in 1950

2. Nation that controlled Korea during World War II

3. Communist section of Korea

4. Geographic area that includes Japan, China, and Korea

5. Capital of South Korea

6. City in which truce talks were held

7. River that separates North Korea from China

8. Place where American forces in the Far East were based

9. Nation that occupied Korea north of the 38th parallel after World War II

10. Name given to South Korea

## IMPORTANT TERMS

1. Solemn declaration against something

2. Person representing a country in the United Nations

3. Tactic that prevents supplies from coming into or out of a seaport

4. Deadlock in fighting

5. The refusal to sign a bill for action in the Security Council

6. System of social organization in which all economic and social activity is controlled by the state

7. Preventing or restricting an enemy's success

8. Nation accused of an unprovoked offensive attack

## PARTICIPANTS IN THE WAR

1. People whose fate was the major problem to be resolved at the cease-fire talks

2. Vehicles used for the first time to carry troops into battle

3. Weapons the Soviet Union supplied to the North Koreans

**5**

**10**

©1978, 1988, 1997, 2002 Walch Publishing

4. Part of the United Nations that decided to send troops to Korea

5. Group that Truman ordered to protect Formosa and to blockade the Korean coast

6. What China claimed its troops in Korea were

9. Technique the communists and North Koreans were accused of using on prisoners to change their thinking

10. War waged with less than total capability or with less than total victory as its purpose

11. Act of sending a person back to his or her own nation

12. Area from which the army has been removed

13. Temporary end of hostilities

14. Term for localized military action with no formal declaration of war, used to describe the Korean conflict

11. Country that occupied Korea south of the 38th parallel after World War II

12. Site of meeting between MacArthur and Truman on October 15, 1950

13. City on which MacArthur ordered an amphibious attack

14. Sea that lies east of the Korean peninsula

15. Strait that separates Korea and Japan

16. Nation that boycotted the Security Council meeting on Korea

17. Nation that sent troops to help the North Koreans

18. City in southern Korea that United Nations forces were pushed back toward

19. Dividing line between North and South Korea

8. This man asked for an emergency meeting of the Security Council after South Korea was invaded.

9. Man whom Mao Tse-tung forced to leave China, along with his followers

10. Man in charge of U.S. troops in Japan

11. Soviet delegate to the Security Council who wasn't there to vote

12. Military leader and civilian leader who clashed over war policies

13. Man who replaced MacArthur as commander of United Nations forces in Korea

15

20

N O T E S

# 30

# The Cold War

## IMPORTANT LEADERS

1. Soviet leader in the early years after World War II

2. Rebel leader who overthrew the government of Cuba and set up a communist government

3. President of the United States during the Cuban missile crisis

4. Communist leader of China after World War II

5. This man replaced President Kennedy as president of the United States.

6. Man who first mentioned the "iron curtain" that separated the free and communist sections of Europe

7. First supreme commander of NATO forces

8. Premier of the Soviet Union during the Cuban missile crisis

## PLACES PEOPLE TALKED ABOUT

1. Capital city of the Soviet Union
2. Communist nation off the coast of Florida
3. Area known for its oil reserves
4. Body of water that the Suez Canal connects to the Red Sea
5. Strait that controls the entrance to the Mediterranean Sea
6. Country of which Indochina was once a colony
7. Nation that controls the Suez Canal

8. Two nations that kept the Soviets from controlling the eastern end of the Mediterranean Sea
9. Jewish nation created after World War II
10. German city surrounded by the Soviet occupation zone after World War II
11. Germany's capital during World War II
12. City that was about three-fourths "free" although it was inside the former communist section of Germany

## EVENTS, GROUPS, AND OBJECTS OF CONFLICT

1. War during which the Soviet Union gained control of eastern Europe

2. Major political party of the Soviet Union

3. Structure built to separate East and West Berlin

4. Organization created to keep peace in the world

5. Product that Cuba sold to the United States before the communist takeover

6. Operation in which the Allied nations flew supplies to Berlin for almost a year

7. Seat of real political power in the Soviet Union

8. Soviet-built weapons whose discovery in Cuba caused a crisis in 1962

9. Middle Eastern waterway that the Soviet Union wanted to control

## TERMS OF CONFLICT

1. Term that describes a period in which two powerful nations distrust each other and use every means of fighting without actually going to war

2. Agreements between nations to help each other in case of attack

3. A ruler who has no respect for individual rights; one who has complete control

4. This prevents goods or supplies from entering or leaving a city.

5. Imaginary barrier that prevented the free exchange of ideas and people between communist and free nations in Europe

6. Idea that communism must be kept within its existing boundaries and must not be allowed to spread

**5**

**10**

©1978, 1988, 1997, 2002 Walch Publishing

7. Countries in eastern Europe that had communist governments and were partly controlled by the Soviet Union

8. A blockade of Cuba was put in place to get the Soviet Union to withdraw missiles it had placed there, which threatened the United States.

9. Chance that an atomic bomb would be dropped on the United States or on one of its allies

10. Term that describes a government with complete control over its citizens

11. Irregular warfare carried on by independent bands or units

12. To force a people to submit to control by an outside force or government

---

10. The Soviet Union won the first lap of the space race with the launching of this satellite.

11. Defense organization formed by nine western European nations plus Iceland, Canada, and the United States to stop the spread of communism

12. Massive parade of soldiers and weapons that took place in Moscow each year

13. Part of the United Nations that condemned the Soviet Union for its actions in Hungary

14. Council or assembly in Russia

15. Soviet Union's answer to NATO

16. Organization formed by the United States and the nations of Latin America in 1948

17. In 1958, Congress formed this in an effort to catch up to the Soviet Union in the space race.

---

13. Area where many political prisoners in the Soviet Union have been sent to work in slave labor camps

14. Neighbor of the Soviet Union not taken over by the U.S.S.R. after World War II

15. Two nations given aid by the United States after World War II to help them fight communism

16. Former communist section of Germany

17. Four nations that divided Germany after World War II and occupied it

18. Geographical area that included Vietnam, Cambodia, and Laos before World War II

19. Former communist European nation that did not follow directions from the Soviet Union

20. Gulf that lies west of the Sinai Peninsula

21. Island to which Chiang Kai-shek's forces fled

22. Communist nation whose people rebelled against Soviet control in 1956, appeared to win, and then were defeated

---

9. Man who ordered the land routes to Berlin closed

10. President in 1965 who sent the marines into the Dominican Republic

11. Secretary of state under Presidents Nixon and Ford

12. This man said, "Ask not what your country can do for you—ask what you can do for your country."

13. First communist leader of the Soviet Union

14. Dictator of Cuba before the communist revolution

15. People who resisted the communists in Hungary

16. First president to visit communist China

**15**

**20**

NOTES

## PEOPLE AND PREJUDICE

1. Settlers from other lands who come to America to live
2. People first brought from Africa in 1619 to work in the colonies
3. Famous African-American leader and clergyman who was assassinated
4. Abolitionist who led a raid on Harpers Ferry
5. Author of *Uncle Tom's Cabin*
6. Famous black leader who said, "I have a dream . . ."

7. People who encountered prejudice when they emigrated because of a potato famine in their native country
8. People in colonial times who agreed to work for a period of time after arriving in America to pay for their passage
9. People who worked openly to end slavery
10. One of the two women who in the 1850s started a national organization to promote women's rights

## LAWS AND GROUPS

1. Organization of whites begun after the Civil War to oppress black people
2. Militant black organization that emerged in the sixties
3. One of the most powerful organizations for women's rights
4. Body of the federal government that deals with Native-American problems
5. Name for Native-American protest movement

6. Organization led by Martin Luther King, Jr.
7. Organization founded in 1910 to help southern African Americans adjust to city life as they moved north
8. Document issued by President Lincoln in 1862 as a step toward freeing the slaves
9. Secret route followed by many slaves fleeing to Canada through the North
10. Organization that has worked for equal rights for African Americans in the twentieth century

## TERMS OF PREJUDICE

1. Class or kind of individuals with common physical characteristics
2. Rights of citizenship that should belong to all citizens
3. More than half of a group
4. Form of protest used by African Americans at segregated restaurants
5. Judging people before knowing them
6. Less than half of a group

7. Separation of races
8. Objecting to something
9. Form of desegregation in which children were sent to schools out of their own neighborhoods
10. Refusal of African Americans to ride segregated buses in an Alabama city

## PLACES PREJUDICE WAS FELT

1. Places in which Native Americans were forced to live
2. Section of the United States where most Mexican Americans live
3. A crowded, run-down apartment house

4. Small factories that have poor working conditions and low wages
5. Part of a city in which members of a minority often live
6. Country where the potato famine occurred, causing many people to emigrate to America

**5**

**10**

©1978, 1988, 1997, 2002 Walch Publishing

7. City in which blacks first refused to ride buses

8. Prison taken over by Native Americans in San Francisco in the 1960s

9. Spanish word for a ghetto or poor section of a large city

10. Camps where Japanese Americans were sent after Pearl Harbor

11. Place where black passengers were once forced to sit on a southern bus

12. Workers who move from farm to farm to harvest crops

---

11. Preconceived ideas about individuals

12. Incorporation as equals into society

13. What the United States has been called because many different nationalities have blended together

14. Unfair or injurious treatment because of race or creed

15. A person who does not have the full rights of citizenship

16. Becoming part of a group; learning a new culture

17. Not belonging; foreign

18. This term means the right to vote.

---

11. Constitutional amendment that outlawed the poll tax

12. Constitutional amendment that outlawed slavery

13. Amendment to allow adult women to vote for president

14. Political party that believed only native-born persons should hold public office

15. Supreme Court decision of 1857 that said African Americans could not be citizens or have rights as citizens

16. Laws that segregated blacks and whites in public places

17. What NAACP stands for

18. Amendment that made African Americans citizens of the United States

19. Act passed in 1964 that guaranteed African Americans equal opportunity in employment

20. Law passed in 1968 that required open housing for all people buying houses or renting apartments

21. Religion of most Irish immigrants

---

11. This African-American woman refused to give up her seat on a Montgomery, Alabama, bus.

12. Native-born Americans who had Japanese ancestors

13. Woman who helped found the National Organization for Women (NOW)

14. What Mexican Americans during the 1960s wished to be called

15. President of the Southern Christian Leadership Conference after Dr. Martin Luther King, Jr. was killed

16. Famous female slave who guided other slaves to freedom in the North

17. Former slave who started a college for African Americans in the South

18. Leader of a rebellion in 1831 against whites in Virginia

19. Well-known Chicano leader of the 1960s and 1970s

20. Famous abolitionist who edited *The Liberator*

21. Runaway slave who wrote the story of his life and became a famous speaker

---

15

20

NOTES

# 32

# The Cities

| CITY DWELLERS | PLACES PEOPLE LIVE AND WORK | CITIES AND GOVERNMENT | GETTING IN AND OUT OF THE CITY |
|---|---|---|---|

1. People who own buildings and rent them to others

2. People who come to America from other countries to live and work

3. Social scientist who studies the ways people live in groups

1. Relating to or characteristic of a city

2. Area on the edge of a city in which many people live

3. Run-down sections of cities

4. Area of a city where minority groups live because of social or economic pressure

5. Places where 95 percent of the people lived during colonial times

6. Parts of a city in which homes are found

1. Money paid by people for the support of their city government

2. People who wish to bring about a change for the better

3. Large city with financial problems that asked the federal government for aid

1. Material that many city streets are paved with

2. Major need of people who live in suburbs but have to work in the city

3. Material that sidewalks are usually made of

---

4. Trained professional, not a mayor, who runs a city

5. President whose New Deal policies were aimed at helping cities during the Great Depression

6. President whose program was called the Great Society

7. Large piece of land set aside for warehouses, office buildings, and factories

8. Central core of a city

9. City and its surrounding residential areas

10. Business areas in the suburbs

11. Enclosed shopping area in which many kinds of stores are located

12. Type of building designed by Americans that provided more office space without using more land

4. Large green area in the middle of Manhattan

5. Congress passed this law to correct air pollution in cities

6. Section of San Francisco that was a hippie center in the 1960s

4. Public transportation that moves many people at once

5. Major highway plan started during the Eisenhower administration

6. Movement of middle-class people to the suburbs

**5**

**10**

 *American History Challenge!*

©1978, 1988, 1997, 2002 Walch Publishing

7. Movement of semiskilled and unskilled workers to the city

8. Form of public transportation run by electricity that took people along city streets to work or shop

9. System of public transportation that carries people underground

10. A railroad that brings workers from the suburbs into the city to work

---

7. City whose Watts section erupted in a bad riot in 1965

8. Northeastern city that had trouble integrating its schools in the 1970s

9. Act with which President Johnson began his "war on poverty"

10. Cabinet-level department established to help correct some of the ills of cities

11. Agency established after the Depression to give middle-class Americans a chance to get home loans

12. Document in which requirements for all new and renovated buildings are found

---

13. Large-scale rebuilding projects of the city

14. Places where people originally moved to be closer to their jobs

15. Large houses in a city divided into many apartments

16. Area of a city in which stores and shops are found

17. Areas of wild or cultivated land provided by cities for recreation

18. Two-family dwelling

19. Group of privately owned but connected homes, the owners of which share in the upkeep of the property

20. Very large urban area made up of several cities

21. Position or place occupied by a building, town, etc.

22. Spanish word for ghetto

---

7. Man who led the Tammany Hall organization and became "Boss" of New York City in the 1800s

8. Woman who started Hull House in Chicago to help the city's poor

9. Famous mayor of New York City during the 1930s

10. America's most distinguished architect

11. Famous architect who invented great domes without inner supports that could cover entire cities

---

15

20

N O T E S

©1978, 1988, 1997, 2002 Walch Publishing

# 33

# How Well Do You Know the Sixties?

| POLITICS | CULTURAL AND PUBLIC EVENTS | RACE RELATIONS | LAW AND CRIME |
|---|---|---|---|

**POLITICS**

1. President who took office in 1961
2. Nation with Soviet missiles that endangered the United States
3. Cuban leader during the missile crisis
4. Nation that cut diplomatic relations with the United States because of problems over a new canal treaty
5. Capital city of North Vietnam, bombed for the first time in 1966
6. European city in which Vietnam peace talks began
7. Man elected president in 1968
8. Volunteer organization established by President Kennedy to help poorer nations
9. Country with which the United States cut diplomatic relations because of problems over the American presence at Guantánamo Bay
10. President who said that American advisors in Vietnam could fire if fired upon
11. Soviet leader during the Cuban Missile Crisis

**CULTURAL AND PUBLIC EVENTS**

1. First American in orbit
2. Name of the first U.S. space program
3. First man to walk on the moon
4. Four mop-haired musicians from England who became famous
5. Extremely short skirts that came into fashion
6. Scottish actor who starred as James Bond
7. World's heavyweight boxing champion who said, "I am the greatest."
8. Television hit of 1967 starring Dan Rowan and Dick Martin
9. Broadway hit that summed up the ideals and protests of the 1960s
10. Man who accomplished the first U.S. suborbital space flight

**RACE RELATIONS**

1. Refusals by African Americans to move from a restaurant until they were served
2. Famous speaker who said, "I have a dream . . ."
3. Man from Massachusetts who was the first African American in 85 years to be elected to the Senate
4. This man worked for farmworkers' rights to form a union.
5. Congress passed this law that made segregation in public places illegal.
6. In 1964, this African-American leader won the Nobel Peace Prize because he used nonviolence to achieve his goals.
7. Man who wrote *Soul on Ice* while in Folsom State Prison
8. Section of Los Angeles where African Americans rioted in 1965
9. Law passed in 1964 that banned discrimination
10. First African American to attend the University of Mississippi

**LAW AND CRIME**

1. What became illegal in 1963 to force children to do in school
2. President who was shot in 1963
3. U.S. senator, presidential candidate, and brother of John F. Kennedy who was shot
4. Illegal drug known as pot
5. Term used when a public figure is murdered
6. Senator investigated for the death of Mary Jo Kopechne, who drowned at Chappaquiddick
7. Assassin of Martin Luther King, Jr.
8. What the Supreme Court ruled all criminal defendants must have

**5**

**10**

9. City in which John Kennedy was assassinated

10. Famous investigation of the Kennedy assassination

11. Dangerous drug used for hallucinatory "trips"

12. Texas fertilizer magnate who was caught selling $24 million in mortgage papers on nonexistent storage tanks

13. Assassin of President Kennedy

14. Man who shot Lee Harvey Oswald

15. City in which Martin Luther King, Jr., was assassinated

16. Assassin of Robert F. Kennedy

11. First African-American U.S. Supreme Court justice

12. Leader who promoted black pride and was killed in 1965

13. First African-American congresswoman

14. African American who introduced the term Black Power

15. Cities in New Jersey and Michigan where race riots occurred

16. Black congressman from New York who lost his seniority for misuse of government funds

17. City where Martin Luther King, Jr., made his famous speech that began "I have a dream . . ."

18. Powerful sect led by Elijah Muhammad

11. Rachel Carson's book that started the environmentalist movement

12. Event in 1969 at which 400,000 young people met to listen to rock and blues music

13. Famous weekly magazine that stopped publishing after 148 years

14. Decade's top team of newscasters

15. Experiments in group living in the 1960s

16. Thin, young model from England who became the rage

17. Artist who helped start the Pop Art movement by painting pictures of Campbell's soup cans

18. President Johnson's dream of new government programs to help citizens

19. Economic period when people can buy less with the money they earn

20. One of the most powerful women's organizations that was started in 1966 by Betty Friedan

12. Only place the Soviet Union and United States agreed nuclear weapons could be tested

13. Resolution by which Congress authorized presidential action in Vietnam

14. Subject of many demonstrations during the sixties

15. Agreement to stop certain kinds of atomic bomb testing

16. Government program established to pay some medical expenses for citizens over age 65

17. To stop the large exodus of citizens, East German authorities built this in 1961.

18. Nation dragged into the Vietnam War in 1966

19. Failed U.S. invasion of Cuba by Cuban exiles

20. What U-2 planes were used for until one was shot down by the Soviet Union

21. Neighbor of Vietnam to which the United States sent military planes

22. Ship with its entire crew that was seized in the Sea of Japan by North Koreans

15

20

NOTES

©1978, 1988, 1997, 2002 Walch Publishing

# 34 The Environment

## CLIMATE AND ATMOSPHERE

1. Average weather conditions of a place
2. Moisture in the form of rain or snow
3. Period when there is a prolonged lack of moisture
4. Thick mist or mass of water droplets floating in the air

5. Mixture of fog and smoke
6. Blanket of air surrounding the earth
7. Gas that is expelled when air is breathed and exhaled
8. Using air movement to generate electricity

## ENVIRONMENTAL TERMS

1. Rare, not common
2. To use our natural environment wisely and without waste
3. Disappearance of a life-form through natural or human causes
4. Unwanted waste that destroys the environment
5. To reprocess something so it can be used again
6. The concern that the earth's supply of fuels is limited
7. Chemicals that kill bugs
8. Life-forms on the brink of disappearance

9. Common term used to indicate hazardous materials
10. Breakdown caused by bacteria
11. Adjustment to environmental conditions
12. Form of interaction in which people or nations must depend on one another to satisfy wants and needs
13. Group of simple plants, often in colonies in the water
14. Matter that settles to the bottom of a liquid

## FARMING AND THE SOIL

1. Method of agriculture in which farmers make ditches to bring water to their crops
2. To prepare and use land to raise crops
3. Planting a field with different crops each year so the land renews itself
4. Hedge or row of trees planted to buffer the force of the wind

5. Farming method in which sections are plowed along ridges or slopes to keep the land from eroding
6. Land that is plowed but left unplanted during the growing season
7. Wearing away of land by wind or water
8. Any chemical used to kill plants

## PEOPLE AND PLACES

1. Number of people in a region or country
2. Person who works with chemical actions and reactions
3. Land area that receives less than 10 inches of rainfall a year
4. Inland bodies of water shared by the United States and Canada

5. Place where people work to make a product
6. Large area in the United States where wheat and corn grow well
7. Nickname for the area in the southwestern United States where severe winds destroyed much land in the 1930s
8. Number of people per square mile

5

10

9. Mixture of pollution and precipitation

10. Layer of the atmosphere that protects us from ultraviolet light

11. Worldwide temperature increase due to depletion of the ozone layer

12. Using the sun's energy as fuel

13. Destroying the forest in this area of South America affects world climate.

---

14. Situation that exists when air near the ground stays cooler than the air above, usually trapping pollution on the surface

15. This nation in southeast Asia is destroying vast forested areas.

16. Automobile exhaust that pollutes the air

---

15. Day set aside each year to call attention to environmental concerns

16. A natural water drainage area

17. An area in or near a community where building can't take place

18. Logging all the trees in an area

19. Smaller system within a larger system

20. A narrow area of vegetation at the edge of or between communities

---

21. Locations for the disposal of nuclear waste and other dangerous materials

22. Natural and physical environment in which all life adapts itself for survival

23. Part of the planet that supports life

24. Supply of something to take care of a need; a natural source of wealth

25. Nonusable parts of production and consumption

26. Practical use of science

---

9. Method of agriculture in which a great deal of work is done on a small amount of land to produce high crop yields

10. Material used by early farmers to build their homes on the Great Plains

11. Often referred to as biotech crops

---

12. Minerals found in the soil that are harmful to plant life

13. Material in the soil derived from living things

---

9. Person who advocates wise use of our resources

10. Person who studies the weather

11. Movement of people from one place to another to make new homes or to find work

---

12. Governmental agency that attempts to cut down pollution

13. Most polluted of the Great Lakes in the sixties

14. This woman wrote *Silent Spring,* a best-selling book telling of problems in the environment.

---

**15**

**20**

**NOTES**

©1978, 1988, 1997, 2002 Walch Publishing

# Women in American History

| WELL-KNOWN WOMEN | WOMEN'S WORK | PLACES AND POLICIES | TERMS INVOLVING WOMEN |
|---|---|---|---|

**TERMS INVOLVING WOMEN**

1. Woman whose husband has died

2. Money or property given by a father to the man his daughter was to marry

3. Women who served in the U.S. Army in World War II were known as this.

4. Women who served in the U.S. Air Force in World War II were known as this.

5. What women have often been called by men who think themselves stronger

6. Right to vote

**PLACES AND POLICIES**

1. American colony where women first arrived in 1619

2. Place where girls were educated in colonial times

3. Proposed amendment approved by Congress in 1970 that was not ratified

4. Rosa Parks became famous for refusing to give this up.

5. Constitutional amendment that gave women the right to vote

6. Section of the nation that allowed women more rights than other sections

**WOMEN'S WORK**

1. Woman who lived with a family and taught their children

2. Woman who helps other women give birth

3. Only acceptable profession for women for many years

4. During wartime, women often helped by doing this.

5. Sandra Day O'Connor was the first woman appointed to this.

6. Organization begun by Jane Addams to improve the lives of the poor

7. Organization founded by Clara Barton during the Civil War

8. Margaret Mead's career

9. Narcissa Whitman went to Oregon in 1836 to do this work.

**WELL-KNOWN WOMEN**

1. Pilot who disappeared in the Pacific

2. Blind and deaf woman whose courage and accomplishments inspired many people

3. Tennis player who beat Bobby Riggs in a controversial and highly publicized match

4. Native American who helped Lewis and Clark

5. A former senator from Maine

6. Former slave who led many people to freedom in the North

7. Woman forced to leave colonial Massachusetts because of religious conflicts

8. Early feminist organizer in America, later honored by a U.S. coin

9. Woman who carried a hatchet and broke up saloons and liquor stores

10. President's wife who became ambassador to the United Nations after her husband's death

11. Athlete and golfer who died of cancer

12. Author of *Uncle Tom's Cabin*

**5**

**10**

7. Nickname for an oral contraceptive

8. During the 1970s and 1980s, women's groups began to push for the right of women to be independent and set their own goals.

9. Not using liquor or using it only a little

10. Offense for which Susan B. Anthony was arrested, tried, and convicted in 1872

11. What women could not legally inherit

12. Garments with whalebone stays that once were fashionable

7. City whose poor were helped by Jane Addams

8. First state in which women could vote

9. State in which Oberlin, the first coeducational college, was founded

10. State in which the first feminist convention, organized by Elizabeth Cady Stanton, was held

11. This statue is of a blindfolded woman with a balance in her hand.

10. Position held by Frances Perkins, the first woman to hold a Cabinet post

11. Profession that opened to women around 1830, one of few acceptable ones

12. Places that Dorothea Dix tried to reform

13. Rose Greenhow's unusual occupation during the Civil War

14. Women who worked for the right to vote

15. Organization that opposed the sale and consumption of liquor

16. Political office for which Margaret Chase Smith ran once

17. In the 1850s, Elizabeth Blackwell became the first woman to do this.

13. First African-American woman to be elected a member of the House of Representatives

14. First woman appointed to the U.S. Supreme Court

15. This woman warned about pesticides killing our environment.

16. The first woman to serve as U.S. Attorney General

17. She was the first female U.S. Secretary of State.

18. Woman who helped Susan B. Anthony in the effort to gain rights for women

19. Designer of knee-length skirts over full pants gathered at the ankle

20. Slave born in New York who became an active abolitionist

21. Nickname for women who worked in industry during World War II

22. She was the first American woman in space.

23. Slave who wrote poetry and wrote letters to George Washington

15

20

NOTES

# The Space Age

# 36

## THOSE WHO DARED

1. Space explorers

2. First men to walk on the moon

3. First American to orbit Earth

4. She was the first American woman in space.

5. A popular movie was made about this space flight crew returning to Earth after an emergency in the lunar module.

6. This 77-year-old U.S. senator revisited outer space in 1998.

## SCENES OF ACTION

1. Site of first landing spot in space for the astronauts

2. Country that launched *Soyuz* space vessels

3. Area from which a rocket is launched

4. Space probes have visited every planet in our solar system except this one.

5. In 1999, this new system containing three planets was discovered by astronomers.

6. Soviet space station that was pulled from orbit in 2001

7. Path around another celestial body

8. State where the launching site for moon shots is located

9. Location of the Mission Control Center for space flights

10. First country to send a satellite into space

## SPACE-AGE VOCABULARY

1. Point or time of landing

2. Getting the spacecraft from the ground into flight

3. Act of picking up a returned spacecraft

4. Act of returning to the earth through the atmosphere

5. Following the movement of a spacecraft

6. The feeling of having little or no gravitational pull

7. Passage of time toward launch

8. Touchdown in the ocean

9. Moment in which a rocket engine fires

10. Time at which a spacecraft leaves the launch pad

11. What astronauts brought from the moon

12. Line of travel through space

13. Interruption in the countdown

## MODERN HARDWARE

1. Name of America's first space flights

2. Human-made object or vehicle intended to orbit a celestial body

3. Beginning in 1998, these two nations developed the International Space Station.

4. These are reusable spacecraft.

5. Protection for a spacecraft from friction heat

6. What *Solar Max* was used to study

7. U.S. spacecraft that carried two astronauts for the first time

8. Spacecraft linked in space with *Soyuz* in 1978

9. Spacecraft that took photos of Jupiter and Saturn

10. Craft with instruments moving through space

11. First human-made satellite to orbit the earth

12. Giant communications satellite developed by American Telephone and Telegraph

13. Apollo spacecraft that was destroyed by fire

14. *Discovery* launched this in 1990 to help astronomers study space.

5

10

©1978, 1988, 1997, 2002 Walch Publishing

©1978, 1988, 1997, 2002 Walch Publishing

15. *Magellan* was launched in 1989 to orbit this planet.
16. Plan to protect the United States from missiles fired by another nation
17. In 1997, the 22-pound *Sojourner* landed on this planet and explored rocks and soil.
18. Nation's first human-occupied space station
19. Name of the first self-piloted ships to land on Mars after photographing the planet
20. First reusable space shuttle
21. Name of the first U.S. satellite

22. System that gives the astronaut an artificial life environment
23. In the *Apollo 15* mission, this vehicle was used to travel on the moon.
24. An unmanned spacecraft landed on this planet but failed to communicate with Earth.
25. This sent back photos of the surface of Mars in 1997.
26. Spacecraft launched in July 2001 to collect atomic particles flowing from the sun

14. Bringing two spacecraft together in space
15. To cancel a mission
16. Safe landing
17. What NASA stands for
18. Speed needed to get away from Earth's gravitational pull
19. Speed of sound
20. Explosive separation of a pilot from a spacecraft

21. Force carrying an object away from the center of rotation
22. Stage in which the rocket booster is discarded
23. Period during a space mission when a spacecraft actively gathers information
24. Period of time during which a spacecraft may be launched to reach a given planet
25. Flow of electrons and protons streaming outward from the sun throughout the solar system

11. Two countries whose spacecraft docked together
12. This planet close to Earth has surface temperatures hot enough to melt lead.
13. This was found near the moon's north and south poles.
14. A space probe discovered that the surface of this planet near Earth is dry and desolate.
15. Area of the moon where Aldrin and Armstrong set down the lunar module

16. This mission exploded 73 seconds after liftoff.
17. Cape Canaveral was called this for a time.
18. Many chunks of ice or rock entering Earth's atmosphere and burning
19. When *Skylab I* fell from orbit, pieces landed on this continent.
20. This prohibited nuclear weapons and weapons of mass destruction in space.

7. President when the first satellite was put into orbit
8. First man to orbit Earth
9. Man known as the Father of American Rocketry
10. One of the three astronauts killed in a cabin fire during on-the-ground training

11. Female teacher who died when the space shuttle *Challenger* exploded
12. Dr. Shannon Lucid spent six months there in 1996.
13. In 1999, Eileen M. Collins became the first woman to command this.
14. In 2001, an American millionaire paid Russia to become the first of these.

**15**

**20**

NOTES

# 37

# Energy

| ENERGY SOURCES | RESOURCE SITES | OIL | ELECTRICITY AND MINING |
|---|---|---|---|

**ENERGY SOURCES**

1. Fuel colonials burned for warmth

2. Sea mammal that supplied fuel for colonial America

3. Endless source of energy

4. Natural movement of the ocean that may be a source of energy

5. Ore required to produce atomic energy

6. Force of nature that can power generators, producing electricity

7. Animals that once supplied power for farmers

**RESOURCE SITES**

1. Body of water off America's southern coast where oil has been found

2. Waterfall between the United States and Canada that became a source of electrical power

3. This nation consumes more primary energy than any other nation.

4. Far northern state in which a large oil field was found

5. Peninsula where a large supply of the world's oil was found

6. South American country with large oil reserves

7. Neighbor of the United States in which huge oil reserves were located in the 1970s and 1980s

8. A number of wind-powered generators in a given location

**OIL**

1. Another name for oil

2. Huge ships built to carry oil

3. Fuel burned by the internal combustion engine

4. Alliance formed by nations to regulate the production and price of oil

5. Facility that changes crude oil into usable oil

6. The United States imports more of this than it produces.

7. Home lighting and heating fuel made from crude oil

8. Oil as it comes from the ground

**ELECTRICITY AND MINING**

1. Electrical power outage

2. These were developed for spacecraft but are now used to make electricity for buildings, watches, and calculators.

3. Coal and natural gas are both used to generate this.

4. When parts of a city or state are deprived of electricity for short periods of time due to power shortages

5. Federal plan that set up dams and electrical plants along the Tennessee River

6. Lack of rain can cut the production of this economical source of electricity.

5

10

©1978, 1988, 1997, 2002 Walch Publishing

7. Digging below ground to extract coal

8. Kind of mining in which huge machines gouge away topsoil to uncover coal below the surface

9. Federal agency that licenses and controls hydroelectric power on public lands

10. Dam on the Colorado River that produces electricity for southern California

11. Kind of mining in which huge machines take a resource from a large hole dug in the land surface

9. Oil well that catches fire

10. Major method of transporting oil across land

11. Poor fuel economy has not stopped buyers from purchasing this popular form of transportation.

12. Area of huge oil deposits along the coast of Alaska

13. Type of rig needed to extract oil from the bottom of large bodies of water

14. Oil-producing nations that cut off America's oil supply in 1973, causing a shortage

15. On February 25, 1991, this nation's northern gulf coastline suffered severe pollution as a result of Iraqi sabotage.

16. This nation spent more than $5 billion to repair oil installations damaged in 1990 by Iraq.

9. This nation produces more primary energy than any other nation.

10. Two states in which large oil-shale reserves have been found

11. State in which America's first oil well was drilled

12. Body of water east of Great Britain where oil was discovered

13. Asian industrial nation dependent on Arabian oil

14. State chosen to research solar energy for the government

15. Country in the Middle East where large oil reserves have not been found

8. Fuel once burned in the steam engine

9. Controversial source of power

10. Energy source that may someday be the cheapest way to heat homes

11. Resource first used to power looms in cloth manufacturing

12. Liquid gas used as rocket fuel in the 1960s

13. Energy supplied by hot springs or geysers

14. In April 1986, an accident occurred in this nuclear power plant, which spread radioactive material over much of Europe.

**15**

**20**

NOTES

©1978, 1988, 1997, 2002 Walch Publishing

# The Vietnam War

# 38

## IMPORTANT PEOPLE

1. Vietnamese leader backed by Chinese communists
2. U.S. president who said that U.S. military advisors would fire if they were fired upon
3. U.S. president who ordered continuous bombing of North Vietnam below the 20th parallel in 1965
4. People who did not want war
5. People who supported the war in Vietnam
6. Man who became president of South Vietnam in 1967
7. U.S. president who sent 35 military advisers to Vietnam in 1950
8. President of the United States when it pulled out of Vietnam

## PLACES ON THE MAP

1. Capital city of North Vietnam
2. Country into which U.S. forces began firing in 1966
3. City in North Vietnam where bombing began in 1966
4. City attacked by communist troops during the Tet Offensive
5. City in which peace talks were carried on
6. Place in which hundreds of civilians were massacred in 1968
7. River that played an important role in the war
8. Capital city of South Vietnam
9. River delta on which the city of Saigon was located
10. European nation that controlled Vietnam before World War II
11. Two communist nations that sent supplies and help to North Vietnam

## TERMS OF WAR

1. Sometimes-violent attempt to overthrow a government
2. Person who flees to a foreign country to escape danger
3. State of wild confusion or disorderly retreat
4. Neutral area separating conflicting forces
5. Policy of preventing the expansion of a hostile power or ideology
6. Person engaged in fighting
7. Avoiding compulsory military service
8. A country that takes no side in a war or conflict
9. Irregular warfare by independent bands of military
10. U.S. troops sent to help train South Vietnamese soldiers

## ITEMS IN THE NEWS

1. North Vietnamese communists
2. What U.S. military personnel went to South Vietnam in 1955 to do
3. Trail used by North Vietnamese soldiers to move supplies and to make attacks on South Vietnam
4. Aircraft that helped evacuate the wounded in Vietnam
5. Parallel at which Vietnam was divided in 1954, giving the communists control of North Vietnam
6. Religious group that denounced the government of South Vietnam in 1963

**5**

**10**

©1978, 1988, 1997, 2002 Walch Publishing

7. Chemical agent used by the United States to destroy vegetation in Vietnam

8. Resolution that authorized presidential action in Vietnam

9. Classified documents on U.S. involvement in Vietnam published by the *New York Times*

10. U.S. merchant ship seized by Cambodian forces in 1975

11. War waged with less than total capability or with less than total victory as its purpose

12. To talk with another nation to arrive at a settlement to a conflict

13. Hostile entrance into a territory

14. President Eisenhower's theory about the spread of communism in Southeast Asia

15. Official postponement of military service

16. Increasing the size and scope of war

17. Area prohibited from being used for military purposes

18. A member of the armed forces whose duties do not include fighting

12. European city where a cease-fire accord was signed between the French and North Vietnam

13. City where 250,000 people marched to protest U.S. involvement in Vietnam

14. Cambodia's capital

15. Place where French forces were defeated and gave up their claim to Vietnam

16. Gulf where North Vietnamese boats reportedly attacked two U.S. destroyers

17. Country into which the Americans and South Vietnamese crossed in April 1970 to attack enemy bases

18. Country invaded by the South Vietnamese for 45 days, aided by U.S. air and artillery forces

19. Area that included Vietnam, Laos, and Cambodia

20. New name for Saigon after the war

21. Gulf that lies off the east coast of Vietnam

9. U.S. president who pardoned most Vietnam War draft evaders

10. Elite U.S. troops specially trained in guerrilla warfare

11. Commander of American forces in Vietnam during the Tet offensive

12. Man who became president of South Vietnam in 1955

13. President when the United States agreed to train South Vietnamese army personnel

14. President of South Vietnam who was assassinated in 1963

15. Man who was court-martialed and convicted of murdering 22 civilians at My Lai

15

20

N O T E S

# 39

# America's Problems in the Middle East

## PEOPLE INVOLVED

1. Israel's first prime minister
2. Leader of Iran before 1979
3. Leader of Egypt who was involved in the Camp David Accords
4. Israeli leader who took office in 1977
5. Leader of Iran during the hostage crisis
6. People who flee to a foreign country for safety
7. People who worship Allah
8. People whose symbol is the Star of David
9. Americans kept against their will for 444 days in Iran
10. Conflict between Palestinians and these people continued to cause unrest in 2002.
11. Leader of Egypt in 1956, during the Suez Canal crisis
12. President who ordered U.S. marines into Lebanon
13. Saudi Arabian leader who was assassinated in 1975
14. King of Egypt overthrown by Nasser

**5**

## PROBLEMS ON LAND

1. Geographic term that describes roughly the area from Libya to Afghanistan
2. Nation that lies west of the Suez Canal
3. Nation that became a homeland for the Jews
4. Holy city captured by Israel in the 1967 war
5. Nation that controls most of the Arabian Peninsula
6. Capital of Egypt
7. City where Iranians attacked the American embassy and took Americans captive
8. Lebanon's capital city
9. Nation requested by Egypt to withdraw its troops from the Suez Canal
10. Where Nasser wanted a dam built
11. Peninsula that lies between the Red Sea and Israel
12. Nation that threatened to enter the 1956 war on Egypt's side
13. Strip of land along the Mediterranean seacoast taken from Israel in the 1950s but reseized by Israel in 1967

## ITEMS IN THE NEWS

1. Temporary stop in the Mideast fighting that is agreed to from time to time
2. Organization that stopped the 1948 war between Israel and the Arabs
3. War that broke out between Israel and two Arab nations in June 1967
4. Raw material that makes the Middle East important to industrialized nations
5. Foreign nationals kidnapped and kept by Islamic militants
6. Empire that included many Middle Eastern nations until World War II
7. Final warning issued by the British and French to Egypt and Israel on October 30, 1956
8. U.S. policy of economic and military aid for Middle Eastern countries, announced in 1957
9. Guerrilla organization working for the freedom of Palestine
10. New type of terrorist attack begun in the 1980s involving individual self-sacrifice

**10**

## PROBLEMS WITH WATER

1. Body of water that connects the Red and Mediterranean seas
2. Major river that flows through Egypt
3. This body of water was badly polluted as a result of the Gulf War of 1991.
4. Body of water off the west coast of Lebanon
5. Body of water that lies west of the Sinai Peninsula
6. Body of water found along Iran's north border

©1978, 1988, 1997, 2002 Walch Publishing

7. Body of water that lies east of the Sinai Peninsula

8. River that became Israel's eastern border after the 1967 war

9. Water route that Nasser seized in 1956

10. The Shatt-Al-Arab waterway is claimed by these two nations, which led to open warfare between them in 1980.

11. Operation Desert Storm forces were used in this conflict in 1991.

12. In September 1993, a peace agreement was signed between Israel and this national faction.

13. War that broke out between the Israelis and the Arabs in 1973

14. Another name for the Central Treaty Organization, a defensive military agreement

15. Agreements about Middle East problems by Sadat, Begin, and President Carter

16. Neutral areas between some hostile Mideast powers

17. A return to a strict religious base for government

18. Iranian militants seized this U.S. site and took Americans hostage

19. Economic measures agreed upon by several nations to force a nation to stop violating international law

14. Nation that controlled Palestine before 1945

15. Two Arab nations attacked by Israel in June 1967

16. Nation that helped Egypt complete the Aswan High Dam

17. An international crisis was sparked when Iraq invaded this nation in 1990

18. Country in which the Golan Heights is located

19. Desert in southern Israel

20. Nation that built the Suez Canal

21. Two nations that joined to form the United Arab Republic in 1958

22. Two nations formed by the division of Palestine

23. Collective farm in Israel

24. A revolution in this country occurred between religious leaders and pro-Western forces.

25. In 1983, 241 U.S. servicemen were killed in a terrorist explosion at their barracks in this nation.

15. Woman who led Israel during the Six-Day War

16. This Egyptian leader was assassinated in 1981.

17. This man led Iraq into the twenty-first century.

18. He was president of the United States during the Gulf War.

19. Saudi Arabia was the home country of this terrorist believed responsible for the September 11, 2001, attacks on the United States.

20. In 2001, the United States sought peace in the Middle East between Israel and these people led by Yasir Arafat.

21. Israel's minister of defense during the Six-Day War

22. Leader of Jordan who asked Great Britain for help

23. Man who promised British aid to establish a Jewish homeland in Palestine

24. He became the leader of the Palestine Liberation Organization (PLO) in 1969.

25. The leader of Israel assassinated in 1996

15

20

N O T E S

©1978, 1988, 1997, 2002 Walch Publishing

# 40

# A Time of Turmoil—The Seventies

## PEOPLE IN THE NEWS

1. Group of people granted the vote by the Twenty-sixth Amendment
2. Man on the inside who "blew the whistle" on the Watergate cover-up
3. First vice president appointed under the provisions of the Twenty-fifth Amendment
4. Man who gave Richard Nixon an unconditional pardon
5. President who resigned before he could be impeached
6. Man who imposed a wage, price, and rent freeze in 1971 in an attempt to slow inflation
7. Wife of Nixon's attorney general who had much to say during the Watergate era
8. Soviet leader who visited the United States in June 1973 and signed cooperation agreements

## WHERE HISTORY WAS MADE

1. Campus where four students were killed when National Guardsmen opened fire during a protest
2. Nation into which the Vietnam War began to spread in 1971
3. North Vietnamese city bombed by the United States during the war
4. State governed by George Wallace
5. City in which the Vietnam peace pacts were signed
6. Communist nation Nixon worked to establish closer ties with
7. Nation whose involvement with the United States was detailed in the Pentagon Papers
8. Nation whose *Soyuz* spacecraft linked up with another craft in space
9. Nation responsible for 1979 ocean oil spill, at that point the worst in history
10. Asian country invaded by the Soviet Union

## ITEMS IN THE NEWS

1. Special day on which millions of Americans demonstrated against pollution
2. Agency no longer controlled by the U.S. government after two centuries as of August 1970
3. Pesticide banned by the Environmental Protection Agency in 1972
4. Resource in short supply during 1973, causing U.S. citizens to wait in long lines
5. Nation's two hundredth anniversary celebration
6. Ship seized by Cambodian forces in the Gulf of Siam
7. Procedure ended by Defense Secretary Laird on January 27, 1973
8. Union whose presidential elections were disrupted by the murder of candidate Joseph Yablonski and his family
9. Newspaper that published the Pentagon Papers

## LAW AND CRIME

1. Lieutenant court-martialed and convicted of murdering civilians at My Lai in Vietnam
2. Vice president who resigned because of tax evasion
3. Man from Texas named special prosecutor in 1973 for the Watergate investigation
4. Name given to the people who broke into the Watergate building
5. Group that opened impeachment hearings against Richard Nixon in 1974
6. Writ commanding a person to appear in court, used often during Watergate
7. Document issued by a president or governor that forgives another person of a crime
8. Budget director and friend of President Carter who was forced to resign
9. Ex-attorney general found guilty of Watergate cover-up and sent to prison
10. Body that ruled Nixon had to turn over the White House tapes

**5**

**10**

©1978, 1988, 1997, 2002 Walch Publishing

**11.** New York prison riot that ended with nine hostages and 28 convicts dead

**12.** Judge in the Watergate case

**13.** Kidnapped daughter of a famous newspaper owner

**14.** This man was found guilty of the slaying of Sharon Tate and six others.

**15.** Two presidential advisers found guilty of helping in the Watergate cover-up

**16.** Federal agency accused of abusing its power because it operated domestically

**17.** Watergate special prosecutor fired by Nixon

**18.** Candidate shot while campaigning in Maryland for the presidency

**19.** Man accused of leaking the Pentagon Papers

---

**10.** Mysterious ailment that killed 29 people who attended a Philadelphia convention

**11.** What the U.S. Senate voted to return to Panama by 1999

**12.** An area from which the army has been removed

**13.** The Supreme Court decision that said a state may not prevent an abortion during the first three months of pregnancy

**14.** Pact signed by President Nixon during summit talks in Moscow in 1972

**15.** Bill passed over Nixon's veto that curbed the president's power to send troops abroad without congressional permission

**16.** New Cabinet-level department created by President Carter

**17.** International oil cartel that raised the price of oil in the 1970s

---

**11.** Site of the first major nuclear reactor accident

**12.** Nation that regained Okinawa by a treaty with the United States

**13.** Communist nation visited by President Nixon in 1972

**14.** Seaport city for Hanoi

**15.** City in which the Kremlin is located

**16.** Mobile missile system approved by President Carter

**17.** Corporation that admitted to bribes of $22 million in order to sell airplanes

**18.** State in which two assassination attempts against President Ford occurred

**19.** Site of a church and trading post captured by the American Indian Movement

**20.** Washington, D.C., building that housed the Democratic National Committee offices

**21.** African country for which Billy Carter registered as an agent, causing his brother, the president, political problems

---

**15**

**9.** President who pardoned the Vietnam War draft-dodgers

**10.** Deposed leader who asked permission to come to the United States to be treated for cancer

**11.** Man who retired after leading the AFL-CIO since 1955

**12.** Secretary of state who resigned because he opposed the attempt to rescue the American hostages in Iran

**13.** Consumer activist who helped citizens against big business

**20**

**14.** This president is credited with opening China in 1972.

**15.** Last name of the Shah of Iran

**16.** Longtime director of the Federal Bureau of Investigation who died

**17.** Democrat from Minnesota who died of cancer after 32 years of public service

NOTES

©1978, 1988, 1997, 2002 Walch Publishing

# The Nation in the Eighties

# 41

## PEOPLE IN THE NEWS

1. Teacher who died aboard the *Challenger*
2. First American woman in space
3. Man elected president of the United States in 1980
4. American president who was wounded in an assassination attempt in 1981
5. This man succeeded Reagan as president.
6. International religious leader wounded in an assassination attempt in Italy in 1981
7. Presidential press secretary wounded in an assassination attempt on the president in 1981
8. Leader of Iran who allowed militants to keep American hostages
9. Longtime leader of Yugoslavia whose death raised the possibility of stronger ties between the U.S.S.R. and Yugoslavia
10. Former head of Ford Motor Company who helped Chrysler repay its debts
11. Anglican Church envoy who attempted to secure release of Americans held in Lebanon
12. Famous movie star whose death from AIDS shocked America

## WHERE HISTORY WAS MADE

1. Volcano that erupted in Washington State
2. City in which American hostages were held for 444 days
3. Site in the Soviet Union of the world's worst nuclear reactor disaster
4. City chosen as the site for the 1988 Summer Olympics
5. This plummeted a record 508 points to set a Dow Jones record.
6. City whose terrorist-related targets were attacked by U.S. warplanes on April 14, 1986
7. Important body of water lying east of Saudi Arabia and controlled by the Strait of Hormuz
8. Country whose oil tankers flew U.S. flags as protection during the Iran-Iraq war
9. African country ruled by Colonel Muammar Al Qaddafi in the 1980s
10. Nation invaded by U.S. Marines and Rangers in 1983
11. A U.S. Navy warship in the Persian Gulf shot down one of this country's commercial airliners

## ITEMS IN THE NEWS

1. Automobile company helped financially by the federal government
2. Most powerful form of cocaine, which is smoked
3. Person held by a group for the release of prisoners or other conditions
4. Place where stocks may be bought or sold in a country
5. Federal government's financial plan that suffered massive deficits in the 1980s
6. Citizens of many nations were exposed to this following the accident at Chernobyl
7. President Reagan and Soviet leader Gorbachev agreed to dismantle all of these with a 300- to 3,400-mile range.
8. Period of intense heat and lack of water which led to one half of agricultural counties being declared disaster areas
9. Proposed constitutional amendment finally defeated after 10 years of effort
10. Pollution problem that was the subject of a U.S.-Canadian agreement in 1986
11. Subject of many talks during the 1980s between the governments of Mexico and the United States

## THE NATION'S HEALTH

1. Major health concern of the 1980s that changed many sexual habits
2. Word meaning "living" or "active" that was applied to a form of exercise popular in the 1980s
3. Change in packaging prompted by deaths caused by cyanide-laced painkillers
4. Key to longer life, said by the *New England Journal of Medicine* in 1986 to significantly diminish the risk of death from all causes
5. Drug of the 1980s, made from coca leaves
6. Cigarette smoke breathed by a nonsmoker
7. Substance in the bloodstream linked in the 1980s to heart disease
8. Surgical removal of eggs from a woman, fertilization in a laboratory, and reimplantation into the woman
9. Legal limit raised by many states in response to congressional backing in 1984
10. Device officially named Jarvik-7 used in the 1980s to prolong life

**5**

**10**

©1978, 1988, 1997, 2002 Walch Publishing

11. Emotional factor causing bodily or mental tension considered in the 1980s as a factor in causing disease
12. Being worn out or uninterested in your job
13. Eighty nations met in Finland to ban harmful substances that are destroying this layer in our atmosphere
14. The U.S. media agreed to carry ads for this product in the fight against AIDS.
15. New method of capital punishment used in the 1980s

16. Improper disposal of waste oil caused this highly toxic chemical to contaminate several sites in Missouri.
17. Substance used in Vietnam that is believed to have caused cancer among many military personnel
18. Mineral that can lessen the weakening of bone mass (osteoporosis), which women became aware of during the 1980s
19. The United States warned home owners of the peril from this odorless gas found in certain soils.

12. Remains of a ship that sank in 1912 explored by scientists
13. Major changes in the way money was collected for the running of the federal government
14. The largest oil spill in U.S. history occurred when this ship struck a reef in Alaska's Prince William Sound.
15. A period of openness between the United States and the Soviet Union
16. Discussions held in Geneva between the Soviet Union and the United States

17. Accident in which seven astronauts died
18. America's first space shuttle
19. This occurred just as the third game of the 1989 World Series began.
20. This scandal plagued the Reagan and Bush presidencies.
21. National newspaper that debuted in the 1980s

13. Powerful Soviet leader of the 1980s who met several times with President Reagan
14. African-American civil rights leader honored by a national holiday
15. Ex-Beatle assassinated in New York City
16. First woman nominated to run for vice president of the United States
17. African-American minister who ran for the Democratic presidential nomination
18. Colonel questioned in the congressional hearings on the Iran-Contra affair

12. In November 1989, the German government announced the opening of this.
13. Mideast nation in which 241 U.S. marines and sailors in a peacekeeping force were killed
14. Country whose racial policies caused the withdrawal of many U.S. firms
15. Nation that helped Americans escape from Iran
16. Site of the 1980 Olympic Games boycotted by the United States

17. Latin American nation with a U.S.-supported government and Soviet-supported guerrillas
18. Country whose Contra rebels were supported by the United States
19. Nation that shot down a South Korean airliner with 269 people on board
20. Site of October 1986 summit meeting between President Reagan and Soviet leader Gorbachev
21. U.S. troops invaded this Central American nation in December 1989.

19. This African-American man was appointed by President George Herbert Walker Bush to serve as chairman of the Joint Chiefs of Staff.
20. Ex-leader of the Philippines who sought U.S. protection after his government was overthrown
21. The ruler of Panama who was indicted for helping the Medellin drug cartel
22. Portion of the U.S. population with the highest percentage increase in the 1980s
23. Chairman of the Federal Reserve Board who directed monetary policies during most of the 1980s

15

20

NOTES

©1978, 1988, 1997, 2002 Walch Publishing

# 42

# The Twentieth Century's Final Decade—Part 1

## HISTORY-MAKING PEOPLE

1. This man led Iraq during the Gulf War.

2. In 1992, this man was elected as forty-second president of the United States.

3. This famous football running back was charged with the killing of his wife and Ron Goldman.

4. This post-war generation began reaching middle age in the 1990s.

5. This former president announced he was suffering from Alzheimer's disease.

6. The case against this man and his involvement in the Iran Contra Affair was dropped.

7. President Clinton appointed this person as head of a task force on health care reform.

8. This Republican became speaker of the House in 1994.

9. This four-time Olympic gold medal winner in diving announced he had AIDS.

10. Lou Gehrig's record of consecutive baseball games played, which was set in 1939, was broken by this player.

## FEATURED ON THE EVENING NEWS

1. The government increased taxes on these items, which led to the phrase "sin taxes."

2. In 1993, a bomb exploded in a parking garage beneath the World Trade Center in this city.

3. The rights each citizen of the United States has

4. The Los Angeles murder trial was called the "Trial of the Century."

5. A bomb ripped through the federal building in this city and state.

6. This man, who many consider the greatest basketball player ever, retired in 1999 and came out of retirement in 2001.

7. According to the FBI, this declined in the closing years of the twentieth century.

8. Spending more than the nation takes in in taxes leads to this economic condition.

9. A riot occurred in Los Angeles in 1992 with the acquittal of four policemen in this famous case.

## FOREIGN RELATIONS

1. Iraq invaded this Middle Eastern nation in 1989, leading to the U.S.'s Operation Desert Storm.

2. Boat refugees came to Florida from this country.

3. Large numbers of U.S. citizens protested when this European nation resumed nuclear testing in the Pacific.

4. Saddam Hussein led this nation in the 1990s and into the twenty-first century.

5. Yitzhak Rabin was the leader of this country until he was assassinated.

6. The world's leading arms dealer

7. Operation Desert Shield was to protect this nation from invasion.

8. Fierce fighting broke out among these three ethnic groups in what was formerly Yugoslavia.

9. The merger of these two nations occurred in 1990.

10. At the White House, Yitzhak Rabin and Yasir Arafat signed an agreement for Palestinian self-rule in this area.

## THE WORLD OF SCIENCE

1. The United States was shocked when Magic Johnson announced he had this disease.

2. The symptoms of this disease include gradual memory loss and physical decline.

3. This is the part of the United Nations that deals with deadly epidemics.

4. Daily doses of this common over-the-counter medicine were found to reduce risk from irregular heart rhythm.

5. The Environmental Protection Agency reported on the depletion of this atmospheric layer.

6. Someone who secretly invades others' computers

7. A person's genetic code

8. Communication device allowing users to speak to others from nearly all locations

9. This allows television users to block certain programs.

10. Smallest unit of information handled by a computer

11. Any error in computer coding or logic

12. These products by Nintendo and Sony are a popular form of entertainment.

**5**

**10**

©1978, 1988, 1997, 2002 Walch Publishing

13. The U.S. Center for Disease Control and Prevention is located here.
14. Nerve gas was released in the subway of this city by terrorists.
15. Many veterans who returned from the Middle East conflict suffered unusual physical ailments called this.
16. Ancient cave art was discovered in this European nation.
17. This man became known as "Doctor Death" because he helped terminally ill patients end their own lives.

18. Largest gathering of national leaders in history took place in this city so leaders could discuss global warming and protection for plants and animals.
19. In 1992, this hurricane devastated south Florida.
20. These chemicals are thought to be most harmful to the ozone.
21. This caused mysterious flulike symptoms that progressed quickly to severe respiratory ailment and death in many victims on or near the Navajo Reservation in the Southwest.

11. An economic agreement among Mexico, the United States, and Canada
12. President Clinton lifted the U.S. trade embargo against this nation in 1993.
13. Even though human right violations continued, the United States continued to renew this nation's most-favored-nation trading status.
14. Refugees from this country were intercepted by the Coast Guard as they tried to enter the United States.

15. The United States sent military troops to this Caribbean nation to restore peace and help prepare for free elections.
16. President Clinton ordered the bombing of a factory in this African nation.
17. U.S. embassies were bombed by terrorists in these two African nations.
18. U.S. military personnel were killed by terrorist bombs in this Middle Eastern nation.
19. Asiatic country accused of violating intellectual property laws regarding U.S. computer software

11. Group of citizens that examines evidence to decide if an accused person should be brought to trial
12. He was found guilty of the Oklahoma City bombing.
13. U.S. president who sent American military forces to Kosovo in 1999
14. This man was approved as associate justice of the Supreme Court despite being accused of sexual harassment.

10. Medical organizations intended to cut the cost of health care
11. Terrorist training camps in this nation were first attacked in 1998 by U.S. missiles in hopes of killing Osama bin Laden.
12. For the first time ever, two men circled the earth nonstop with this.
13. Laws were passed and proposed dealing with the selling, owning, and use of these.
14. Term describing the difficulty women have in reaching top corporate jobs

15. Attempt to remove all people who are not of a certain ethnic background
16. This central bank controls the interest rate in the United States.
17. Navy sex scandal that erupted at a convention in 1991 in the Las Vegas Hilton
18. Seven people who served the White House in this office were fired by the Clinton administration for "gross mismanagement," only to be found innocent later.
19. A mother and son died during this stand-off with the FBI in Idaho.

15. This famous gun control bill was passed bearing the name of the man who was shot at the same time as President Reagan.
16. Aldrich Ames was a longtime Soviet spy in this U.S. agency.
17. This heavyweight boxer served three years in prison for rape.
18. Independent counsel who investigated President Clinton
19. She was the first female U.S. secretary of state.

15

20

NOTES

# 43

# The Twentieth Century's Final Decade—Part 2

## HISTORY-MAKING PEOPLE

1. He was a former president who met with warring factions in Bosnia to try to bring peace.

2. Name given by the FBI to the person who mailed bombs to his victims beginning in 1978

3. Judge who became famous in the O.J. Simpson trial

4. Friends and associates of this president were involved in major campaign finance scandals.

5. The Americans with Disabilities Act was signed by this president.

6. This man became important in the 1992 presidential election when he formed a third political party.

7. This black leader was freed by South Africa after 27$\frac{1}{2}$ years in jail.

8. A person who complains to outside authorities about wrongdoing in his or her company

9. He was only the second U.S. president to be impeached.

10. This man led the Branch Davidians in Waco, Texas.

## FEATURED ON THE EVENING NEWS

1. Twenty-seven rounds were fired at this structure in an attempt to assassinate President Clinton.

2. In 1995, the nation watched as rescuers tried to find buried people after a 7.2 earthquake hit this Asian nation.

3. An economic condition in which the income of a nation equals the outgo or spending of that nation

4. The Northridge section of this American city was struck by an earthquake, killing 61 people.

5. The "Great Flood of 1993" surged down this river and its tributaries.

6. Arkansas land scandal that plagued President Clinton

7. This capital of Yugoslavia was almost destroyed in fighting.

8. U.S. forces joined NATO forces to act as peacekeepers in this former part of Yugoslavia.

9. Firing or laying off employees to show greater profit

10. Policy giving hiring preference to members of racial minorities

## FOREIGN RELATIONS

1. A formal agreement between nations that is like a treaty is called this.

2. More than 120 countries signed an agreement that forbade the making, stockpiling, or use of these types of weapons.

3. Most illegal immigrants entering the United States came from this nation.

4. The United States did not pay some of its dues to this international organization.

5. In 1999, the United States returned control of this canal to the nation it crosses.

6. The United Nations peacekeepers saved millions of people from famine but were unable to establish a stable government in this African nation.

7. This famous battleship pounded Iraqi targets and helped end the Persian Gulf War.

8. This huge nation negotiated with the United States to enter the World Trade Organization.

9. Economic sanctions were imposed against this nation following the Gulf War.

## THE WORLD OF SCIENCE

1. The premature termination of the life of a fetus

2. This disease continued to spread rapidly through world populations.

3. This corporation that made silicon gel implants was sued by women with health problems.

4. This popular movie was about using DNA to re-create dinosaurs.

5. The vast computer network

6. Real-time, on-line discussion groups where people can communicate from their computers

7. Computer program that performs a specific task

8. The on-line world of computer networks

9. This soybean food additive is an excellent source of protein.

10. Device known as GPS, which gives the location of any site on Earth through use of satellites

11. A warming of Pacific waters that causes major weather changes

12. The most modern airport in the United States that opened in the 1990s

**5**

**10**

©1978, 1988, 1997, 2002 Walch Publishing

**15**

11. The Twenty-seventh Amendment was proposed by this man and took almost two hundred years to get ratified.

12. This woman became Attorney General of the United States in 1993.

13. The death of this man who was deputy White House counsel and a close friend to President and Mrs. Clinton was ruled a suicide.

14. The nation watched videotape of this man being beaten by police in Los Angeles.

11. Citizens in this U.S. possession voted against trying to become a state.

12. High school in Colorado where the mass shooting of fellow students by two boys shocked the world

13. Lawsuits filed against this industry by federal and state governments resulted in billion-dollar settlements.

14. Amendment to the Constitution regarding pay raises in Congress

15. Four federal agents were killed in an attack on the Branch Davidian compound located in this city and state.

10. The United States and European nations criticized this Asian nation for its restrictive policy on imports.

11. This religious movement in the Middle East brought in a religious leader as the president of Iran.

12. A U.S. army reconnaissance helicopter was shot down by this Asian nation.

13. A loose network of documents that are connected through hyperlinks

14. The largest land conservation bill ever passed for the United States outside Alaska

15. This deadly virus that has no cure appeared in Zaire in 1995, frightening the world's nations.

16. Changing the expression of a person's genes to treat, cure, or prevent disease

**20**

15. White House aide romantically linked with President Clinton

16. This man headed the Federal Reserve Board and was reappointed by President Clinton in 1996.

17. This leader of Sinn Fein, the political wing of the Irish Republican Army, came to the United States to discuss Irish problems with President Clinton.

18. Commerce secretary who was killed in a plane crash in Bosnia

16. Federal elections held two years after presidential elections

17. Any scheme that causes profits from illegal activities to appear legitimate

18. Tax passed in 1990 on expensive jewelry, furs, autos, and boats

19. Gives the president power to veto single items in the budget

20. The use of confidential information to make money on the stock market

13. What GATT stands for in the GATT Treaty, an economic agreement with Europe

14. This was the subject of an international conference in Kyoto, Japan.

17. Location in which terminally ill patients can spend their final days

18. Colder-than-normal sea-surface temperatures in the tropical Pacific

19. Scientists worked on this to identify all the human genes.

20. These convert sunlight into electricity.

21. For the first time ever, it defeated a chess grandmaster in 1997.

N O T E S

## PEOPLE

1. Local law that prohibits children and youth from being on the streets after a given hour

2. Term describing violence because of traffic situations

3. In 2000, he became the first U.S. president found in contempt by a federal court.

4. A progressive degenerative brain disease becoming more common as people live longer

5. Potentially fatal hallucinogenic drug popular among those attending raves

6. This self-described "Cablinasian" golfer won both the Masters and the U.S. Open.

7. In the 2000 U.S. presidential election, this tiny bit of punched paper became a household word.

8. A school or district policy requiring punishment for specific offenses, regardless of circumstances

9. Illegal immigrants often work in these shops or factories at low wages.

## THE ECONOMY

1. This coin issued in 2000 failed to gain popularity.

2. Energy problems in this state warned the entire nation of possible future difficulties.

3. It rose to over 11,000 in 2000 before falling.

4. What a person or family must spend in order to live

5. Not having enough income to provide for basic needs

6. Percent of workers without jobs

7. A 12-month accounting period that may or may not begin in January

8. A time of falling stock prices

9. The term "plastic money" refers to this.

10. The stock exchange on which the most technology stocks are traded

11. A time of rising stock prices

12. The Bush administration proposed an increase in oil exploration in a huge wildlife conservation area in this state.

## U.S. AND WORLD RELATIONS

1. Holding hostages for money to finance extremist groups

2. Even though the Cold War is over, some FBI and CIA agents have been accused of this.

3. American schoolchildren raised money in 2000 and 2001 to buy the freedom of these people in Africa.

4. The United States sponsored peace talks between Palestine and this nation.

5. The United States began paying some of its back dues to this world organization.

6. U.S. president who declared war on terrorism

7. Those who tried to flee Afghanistan to escape the Taliban, U.S. bombs, and starvation

8. New York City financial center destroyed by terrorists on September 11, 2001

9. Nation from which terrorist Osama bin Laden operated in 2001

10. The United States is trying to help this continent with the greatest number of citizens infected with HIV and AIDS.

## SCIENCE AND TECHNOLOGY

1. To prevent counterfeiting, the U.S. Treasury redesigned this.

2. An SPF number is important in preventing this disease.

3. Artificial environment created by a computer

4. Many falsely imprisoned people have been freed using this technology.

5. Nickname for Internet stocks

6. Many older people suffer from this disease, which results in porous, brittle bones.

7. Nucleic acid that contains genetic information in all organisms

8. Computer science dealing with computers acting like humans

9. A computer application that lets a user view files on the World Wide Web

10. Leading cause of death in the United States

11. Security system designed to protect a computer system

12. Fuel-efficient cars powered by both gas engines and electric motors

**5**

**10**

10. Binge eating, usually ending with self-induced vomiting
11. This son of a former U.S. president was killed when his plane crashed at sea.
12. He became the first African-American U.S. secretary of state.
13. According to the 2000 census, this is the fastest-growing ethnic group in the United States.
14. American cyclist who overcame cancer to win the Tour de France
15. The new millennium actually began in this year.

16. This private foundation spent more in 2000 to improve health in poor nations than did the U.S. government.
17. According to the 2000 census, this section of the United States had the most counties that lost population in the previous ten years.
18. Term used to describe television programs such as *Survivor* and *The Real World*
19. The U.S. Supreme Court ruled that this protective act applies to professional golfers.

**15**

13. This term is used when a company asks consumers to return a defective product for replacement or a refund.
14. In June of 2000, a federal judge ordered this software company to be split into two companies.
15. Loss of one's property because mortgage payments were not made
16. This industry controls the nation's local telephone access links.
17. The difference in pay between men and women

18. When first written in 1913, it was 14 pages long, but now contains thousands of pages and hundreds of different forms.
19. Having to pay more income tax as a couple than two single people with similar incomes
20. Economic expansion resulted in a surplus in this for the first time in many years.
21. When tax collections increased dramatically, this declined.

11. Nation that accepted several million refugees from Afghanistan
12. In the fall of 2001, these disease spores were sent by mail, causing illness and death.
13. The future status of this city in the Middle East brought a halt to the Mid-East Summit at Camp David in 2000.
14. This nation agreed to pay damages to Jewish people used as slave laborers in World War II.
15. A U.S. spy plane crash-landed here in 2001.

16. Illegal immigrants from Mexico pay these people to help them enter the United States.
17. The use of bacteria or viruses to spread fear and kill people
18. Terrorist Osama bin Laden was educated in these two Western nations.
19. Washington, D.C., airport that remained closed longer than other airports after the September 11, 2001, terrorist attacks

**20**

13. In 2001, U.S. agricultural officials feared that this disease of sheep, cattle, and hogs might spread from Europe.
14. A person other than a company employee who checks new computer products such as software before their final release
15. Nontraditional methods of treating disease and illness
16. A wasting disease affecting deer in the western United States is similar to this fatal disease affecting cattle in Europe.

17. These types of genes are thought to determine alertness in the morning and sleepiness at night.
18. This subatomic particle was proved to have mass, thereby accounting for a large percent of the "missing mass" in the universe.
19. Scientists were finally able to transport this faster than the speed of light.
20. Atomic clocks finally were able to measure time in these divisions.

**NOTES**

©1978, 1988, 1997, 2002 Walch Publishing

# 45 | Into the New Millennium—Part 2

## PEOPLE

1. Gender more likely to vote in a presidential election

2. She was the first former first lady to be elected to the U.S. Senate.

3. The outcome of the 2000 presidential election hinged on ballot recounts in this state.

4. This count of the population of the United States happened in 2000.

5. Excess food and lack of exercise contribute to this major health hazard.

6. As more Americans become obese, this disease frequently treated with insulin is becoming more common.

7. Workers without this generally have the highest rates of unemployment.

8. This famous African-American female talk show host started a book club that encouraged millions of people to read.

9. One who illegally and improperly follows and watches another person

10. He lost the 2000 presidential election to George W. Bush.

**5**

**10**

## THE ECONOMY

1. In an effort to stimulate the economy, Congress passed a law in 2001 giving a one-time refund to all who paid income taxes.

2. Excessive credit-card debt causes many to declare this.

3. Retirees cannot depend on this government pension to pay for all their needs.

4. Firing employees in an effort to increase company profits

5. Drought in the Pacific Northwest cut the production of this energy source.

6. Plastic card that instantly withdraws money from the cardholder's bank account

7. This group may increase interest rates in an effort to avoid or fight inflation.

8. A temporary shutoff of electrical power that moves from one place to another

9. Tires manufactured by this company were blamed for many fatal roll-over accidents.

10. Federal Reserve chairman who had great economic power at the start of the new millennium

## U.S. AND WORLD RELATIONS

1. Much of the cocoa for chocolate grown in the Ivory Coast is picked by this kind of labor.

2. Government building hit by an airplane in the September 11, 2001, terrorist attack on Washington, D.C.

3. Two New York City skyscrapers hit and destroyed by airplanes in the September 11, 2001, terrorist attack

4. Following the terrorist attacks of September 11, 2001, these were closed by the FAA for several days.

5. In October of 2001, this Irish organization said it would disarm.

6. These religious rulers in Afghanistan opposed U.S. policies and sheltered international terrorists.

7. In 2000, the United States established normal trade relations with this huge nation.

8. Western defense organization that agreed the attacks on the World Trade Center in 1993 and 2001 were linked to the U.S. embassy attacks in East Africa

## SCIENCE AND TECHNOLOGY

1. The information highway

2. Small portable computer

3. Unsolicited e-mail messages sent to many

4. This is known as WWW.

5. An increase in skin cancer is partly due to a reduction in this.

6. This may cause a rise in the levels of the world's oceans.

7. An exact copy of an animal produced by genetic engineering

8. A DNA segment that creates a trait

9. In 2001, this space station was declared obsolete.

10. DNA that contains genes from different sources that have been combined

11. Project for which the United States and Russia cooperated in building a permanent platform in space

12. Drugs that fight inflammation without damage to the stomach

©1978, 1988, 1997, 2002 Walch Publishing

13. Nonsteroidal anti-inflammatory drugs, including aspirin

14. Emissions that come from burning fossil fuels

15. Plants altered by transfer of genes

16. Encoding computer data to keep it secret

17. Conclusive evidence for the existence of water on this "red planet" was discovered in the year 2000.

18. Scientists proved that humans can be influenced by these hormones, which can be smelled on other people.

19. NASA landed the NEAR spacecraft on this asteroid.

20. Scientists were able to detect this on extrasolar planets.

21. Scientists were able to stop light from doing this by sending it through laser-lit vapors.

9. During 2000, this measure of foreign trade was the worst in U.S. history.

10. Violent demonstrations took place when members of this trade organization met.

11. The United States signed a trade agreement with this 1960s enemy nation.

12. Nations such as Russia and China criticized U.S. plans to build this missile defense system.

13. The United States continued to enforce no-fly zones set up in this nation after the Gulf War.

14. Mayor of New York City when the twin towers at the World Trade Center were destroyed

15. Terrorist group headed by Osama bin Laden

11. Marketing of goods or services by telephone

12. Extremely high interest loans made to cash-poor workers for a week or two

13. The time between a credit card purchase and the date payment must be made to avoid interest charges

14. All taxes paid, including federal income tax, sales tax, Medicare tax, Social Security, property tax, license taxes, state or city income tax, etc.

15. Difference between the earnings of low-wage earners and higher-earning workers

16. To stimulate the economy, the Federal Reserve may cut these.

17. They make many stock market sales and purchases for themselves each day.

11. Computer users visit these real-time, on-line discussion groups to communicate about items of interest.

12. Voters in some states approved the use of this illegal drug for medical purposes.

13. For the first time ever, a blind man climbed this mountain.

14. Outdoor activities or forms of sport that involve a high degree of physical risk

15. Gender of students receiving the most college degrees

16. Voters in some states made this legal, allowing doctors to help terminally ill patients die.

17. This six-year-old Cuban boy rescued at sea became a top news story when he was forced to return to Cuba.

18. Appointed by President George W. Bush, she was the first African-American female to be national security adviser.

19. Those who work at home and use a computer to connect to their office

20. He is only the second U.S. president who is the son of a former U.S. president.

15

20

NOTES

©1978, 1988, 1997, 2002 Walch Publishing

# Answer Key

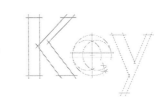

# 1 Concepts in History

| | History Makers | Historical Locations | Historical Times | Ideas Important to History |
|---|---|---|---|---|
| **5** | 1. What are historians?<br><br>2. What is an eyewitness? | 1. What is a frontier?<br><br>2. What were colonies? | 1. What is a calendar?<br><br>2. What is prehistoric time?<br><br>3. What is a century?<br><br>4. What is the birth of Christ? | 1. What is a treaty?<br><br>2. What is religion?<br><br>3. What is government?<br><br>4. What is a peace treaty? |
| **10** | 3. What are events?<br><br>4. What is an archaeologist? | 3. What is an empire?<br><br>4. What was the New World? | 5. What is a decade?<br><br>6. What was the Iron Age?<br><br>7. What is *Anno Domini*?<br><br>8. What is an epoch? | 5. What is a government?<br><br>6. What is an invasion?<br><br>7. What is overpopulation?<br><br>8. What are civil wars? |
| **15** | 5. What is an ally?<br><br>6. What is *Homo sapiens*? | 5. What were river valleys?<br><br>6. What is a landform? | 9. What is an era?<br><br>10. What is a score?<br><br>11. What was the Stone Age?<br><br>12. What is a millennium? | 9. What is evidence?<br><br>10. What is research?<br><br>11. What is a theory?<br><br>12. What is a quotation?<br><br>13. What is civilization? |
| **20** | 7. What are barbarians?<br><br>8. What is heritage (or culture)? | | 13. What is an eon?<br><br>14. What is a generation? | 14. What is economy?<br><br>15. What is a dynasty?<br><br>16. What is imperialism?<br><br>17. What is an artifact? |

# 2  Geographic Concepts

| | General Geographic Terms | Landform Terms | Bodies of Water | Geographic Pinpoints |
|---|---|---|---|---|
| **5** | 1. What is an atlas?<br><br>2. What is a globe?<br><br>3. What is a hemisphere?<br><br>4. What is the equator?<br><br>5. What is climate? | 1. What are landforms?<br><br>2. What is a continent?<br><br>3. What are plains?<br><br>4. What is a peninsula?<br><br>5. What is a volcano?<br><br>6. What is an island? | 1. What is a stream?<br>2. What is the Atlantic Ocean?<br>3. What are the Great Lakes?<br>4. What is the Gulf of Mexico?<br>5. What is the Mississippi River?<br>6. What is San Francisco Bay? | 1. What is the North Pole?<br>2. What is New Orleans?<br>3. What is Chicago?<br>4. What is Rhode Island?<br>5. What is Canada?<br>6. What is Texas?<br>7. What is the South Pole? |
| **10** | 6. What is geography?<br><br>7. What is precipitation?<br><br>8. What is a gazetteer?<br><br>9. What is the equator?<br><br>10. What is silt? | 7. What is a mountain range?<br><br>8. What is a desert?<br><br>9. What is a canyon?<br><br>10. What is a cape?<br><br>11. What is a cliff?<br><br>12. What is a plateau? | 7. What is the Rio Grande?<br><br>8. What is the Arctic Ocean?<br><br>9. What is a bay?<br><br>10. What is a canal?<br><br>11. What is a river mouth? | 8. What is the Appalachian Range?<br>9. What is Cape Cod?<br>10. What is New York City?<br>11. What is Alaska?<br>12. What is Juneau?<br>13. What is Mexico?<br>14. What is Maryland? |
| **15** | 11. What is a rain forest?<br><br>12. What is a cartographer?<br><br>13. What is upstream?<br><br>14. What is latitude?<br><br>15. What is a glacier? | 13. What is a delta?<br><br>14. What are the Great Plains?<br><br>15. What is a fall line?<br><br>16. What is a basin?<br><br>17. What are coastal plains? | 12. What is a reservoir?<br>13. What is Chesapeake Bay?<br>14. What is the Ohio River?<br>15. What is the Great Salt Lake?<br>16. What is the Columbia River?<br>17. What is the Gulf of Alaska? | 15. What is Alaska?<br>16. What are the Florida Keys?<br>17. What are the Rocky Mountains?<br>18. What is the Cascade Range?<br>19. What is San Francisco?<br>20. What is Hawaii? |
| **20** | 16. What are wetlands?<br>17. What are foothills?<br>18. What is the Piedmont?<br>19. What is the prime meridian?<br>20. What are parallel lines?<br>21. What is the Arctic Circle? | 18. What is an isthmus?<br><br>19. What is a prairie?<br><br>20. What is tundra?<br><br>21. What is a mesa?<br><br>22. What is a marsh (or swamp)? | 18. What is a strait?<br>19. What is a channel?<br>20. What is a fjord?<br>21. What is a tributary?<br>22. What is the Colorado River?<br>23. What is the Erie Canal?<br>24. What are the Everglades?<br>25. What is the Bering Strait? | 21. What is Long Island?<br>22. What is the Alaska Range?<br>23. What is the Mojave Desert?<br>24. What is the Ozark Plateau?<br>25. What is Cape Hatteras? |

# 3  The Exploration Period

| | Those Who Dared | Places of Importance | Things Important to the Explorers | Geographic Pinpoints |
|---|---|---|---|---|
| 5 | 1. Who were the Vikings?<br>2. Who was Isabella?<br>3. Who was Balboa?<br>4. Who was Hernando Cortés?<br>5. Who was John Cabot? | 1. What was Spain?<br>2. What was San Salvador?<br>3. What was Spain?<br>4. What was Florida?<br>5. What were the Philippines?<br>6. What was Mexico? | 1. What were gold and silver?<br>2. What were the *Niña, Pinta,* and *Santa Maria?*<br>3. What was silk?<br>4. What was a colony?<br>5. What was Christianity? | 1. What was the Gulf of St. Lawrence?<br>2. What was the Atlantic Ocean?<br>3. What was the Fountain of Youth?<br>4. What is a strait?<br>5. What was the South Sea? |
| 10 | 6. What was Indian?<br>7. Who was Sir Francis Drake?<br>8. Who was Sieur de LaSalle?<br>9. Who were Louis Jolliet and Father Jacques Marquette?<br>10. Who was Jacques Cartier? | 7. What was South America?<br>8. What was the Cape of Good Hope?<br>9. What were the East Indies?<br>10. What was Newfoundland?<br>11. What was Brazil? | 6. What is navigation?<br>7. What is an expedition?<br>8. What was the mother country?<br>9. What were horses?<br>10. What were horses and guns? | 6. What was the Mississippi?<br>7. What was the St. Lawrence?<br>8. What was the Mississippi?<br>9. What was the Indian Ocean?<br>10. What was the Pacific? |
| 15 | 11. Who was John Cabot?<br>12. Who was Hernando de Soto?<br>13. Who was Francisco Pizarro?<br>14. Who was Hernando Cortés?<br>15. Who was Ferdinand Magellan?<br>16. Who was Ponce de Leon? | 12. What were the Bahamas?<br>13. What was Spain?<br>14. What was Peru?<br>15. What was Portugal?<br>16. What was Hispaniola?<br>17. What were Spain and Portugal? | 11. What was a compass?<br>12. What was scurvy?<br>13. What was the Line of Demarcation?<br>14. What was the *Santa Maria?*<br>15. What was the *Victoria?* | 11. What is the Strait of Magellan?<br>12. What was the Mississippi?<br>13. What was Hudson Bay?<br>14. What was San Francisco Bay? |
| 20 | 17. Who was Ponce de Leon?<br>18. Who was Francisco Coronado?<br>19. Who was Samuel de Champlain?<br>20. Who was Juan Cabrillo?<br>21. Who was Pedro Cabral?<br>22. Who was Giovanni da Verrazano? | 18. What was Mexico City?<br>19. What were the Andes?<br>20. What was the Isthmus of Panama?<br>21. What was Palos, Spain?<br>22. What were France, England, and Spain? [Name two.] | 16. What was the *Golden Hind?*<br>17. What were the Seven Cities of Cibola?<br>18. What was the Northwest Passage?<br>19. What is a journal?<br>20. What is a pueblo? | 15. What were the Atlantic, Pacific, and Indian?<br>16. What was the Sea of Darkness?<br>17. What were the Grand Banks?<br>18. What is the Caribbean Sea? |

# 4 The Colonial Period

| | Colonial Personalities | Where in the World? | Items of Interest | Colonial Ideas and Beliefs |
|---|---|---|---|---|
| 5 | 1. Who was Sir Walter Raleigh?<br>2. Who was John Smith?<br>3. Who was James Oglethorpe?<br>4. Who was William Penn?<br>5. Who was Myles Standish?<br>6. Who was John Peter Zenger? | 1. What was Roanoke?<br>2. What was Plymouth?<br>3. What was Jamestown?<br>4. What was Cape Cod?<br>5. What was Georgia?<br>6. What was Virginia?<br>7. What was Viginia? | 1. What was gold?<br>2. What was the *Mayflower*?<br>3. What was the mosquito?<br>4. What were fish?<br>5. What was farming?<br>6. What was tobacco?<br>7. What was a charter? | 1. What was trade?<br>2. What was religious freedom?<br>3. What was self-government? |
| 10 | 7. Who was John Winthrop?<br>8. Who were Samoset and Squanto?<br>9. Who was Pocahontas?<br>10. Who was Roger Williams? | 8. What was Massachusetts?<br>9. What was Massachusetts Bay?<br>10. What was Maryland?<br>11. What was France?<br>12. What was New Amsterdam?<br>13. What was Manhattan?<br>14. What was Fort Christina? | 8. What was "Croatoan"?<br>9. What was Lord Baltimore?<br>10. What was the Mayflower Compact?<br>11. What was fur?<br>12. What was the Bible?<br>13. What were stocks, pillory, and dunking stool? [Name two.] | 4. What was the Church of England (or Anglican Church)?<br>5. What was (Roman) Catholic?<br>6. What was freedom of the press? |
| 15 | 11. Who was James I?<br>12. Who was Elizabeth I?<br>13. Who was John Rolfe?<br>14. Who was William Bradford?<br>15. Who was Peter Minuit?<br>16. Who was Virginia Dare? | 15. What was St. Augustine?<br>16. What was Massachusetts?<br>17. What was Philadelphia?<br>18. What was Santa Fe?<br>19. What was Holland? | 14. What was a hornbook?<br>15. What was the London Company?<br>16. What was the House of Burgesses?<br>17. What was the Toleration Act?<br>18. What was the "starving time"?<br>19. What were the Fundamental Orders of Connecticut? | 7. What was representative government?<br>8. What was rule by majority?<br>9. What is a humanitarian?<br>10. What was religious freedom? |
| 20 | 17. Who was Peter Stuyvesant?<br>18. Who was John Carver?<br>19. Who was Anne Hutchinson?<br>20. Who was Charles II?<br>21. Who was Nathaniel Bacon?<br>22. What was a viceroy? | 20. What is New York City?<br>21. What was Hartford, Connecticut?<br>22. What was Providence, Rhode Island?<br>23. What was New Jersey?<br>24. What were New England, the Middle colonies, and the Southern colonies?<br>25. What were the Grand Banks? | 20. What was triangle trade?<br>21. What were town meetings?<br>22. What were the Navigation Acts?<br>23. What was Parliament?<br>24. What was the *New England Primer*?<br>25. What was chocolate? | 11. What was a veto?<br>12. What was separation of church and state?<br>13. What were missionaries? |

## 5 | Colonial Life

| | Who Lived in the New World? | Somewhere in the New World | Things Important to the Colonists | Water Bodies the Colonists Knew |
|---|---|---|---|---|
| **5** | 1. Who were the Native Americans?<br><br>2. What were blacksmiths?<br><br>3. What was a master?<br><br>4. What were slaves?<br><br>5. What were indentured servants? | 1. What were the New England colonies?<br><br>2. What were the Southern colonies?<br><br>3. What was the frontier? | 1. What was corn?<br><br>2. What was a canoe?<br><br>3. What was a mill?<br><br>4. What was a horse?<br><br>5. What was farming?<br><br>6. What was tobacco? | 1. What was the Atlantic Ocean?<br><br>2. What was Massachusetts Bay?<br><br>3. What was the Atlantic Ocean?<br><br>4. What was the James River?<br><br>5. What was the Hudson River? |
| **10** | 6. What were boys?<br><br>7. What was Quaker?<br><br>8. What were craftsmen?<br><br>9. What were tradesmen?<br><br>10. Who were the Huguenots? | 4. What are plantations?<br><br>5. What was the wilderness?<br><br>6. What was England? | 7. What was a sampler?<br>8. What was indigo?<br>9. What were rice, tobacco, indigo, and cotton? [Name three.]<br>10. What was shipbuilding (or fishing)?<br>11. What was maple?<br>12. What were snowshoes? | 6. What was Delaware Bay?<br><br>7. What was the Connecticut River?<br><br>8. What were the Grand Banks?<br><br>9. What was Chesapeake Bay?<br><br>10. What was Lake Champlain? |
| **15** | 11. Who were the Swedes?<br><br>12. What were women?<br><br>13. Who were the Puritans?<br><br>14. Who were the Pilgrims? | 7. What were the Appalachians?<br><br>8. What were the Middle colonies?<br><br>9. What is Newfoundland? | 13. What was iron?<br>14. What was wool?<br>15. What was whaling?<br>16. What was a log cabin?<br>17. What was pork?<br>18. What was a dame school? | 11. What was Long Island Sound?<br><br>12. What was Chesapeake Bay?<br><br>13. What was the Mohawk River?<br><br>14. What was Narragansett Bay?<br><br>15. What was the Savannah River? |
| **20** | 15. What were proprietors?<br><br>16. What were coopers?<br><br>17. Who were the Iroquois?<br><br>18. What were immigrants?<br><br>19. What was the overseer? | 10. What was Nantucket?<br><br>11. What is a common (or village green)?<br><br>12. What is a town meeting?<br><br>13. What is Cape Hatteras? | 19. What was linen?<br>20. What were naval stores?<br>21. What were duties?<br>22. What was an assembly?<br>23. What was the militia?<br>24. What were cash crops?<br>25. What was the mercantile system? | 16. What is the Connecticut River?<br><br>17. What was the Delaware River?<br><br>18. What is a tidewater? |

# 6 The French and Indian War

| | Important People | Important Locations on Land | Important Things and Ideas | Important Locations on Water |
|---|---|---|---|---|
| **5** | 1. Who was George Washington?<br><br>2. Who was Edward Braddock?<br><br>3. Who was Daniel Boone? | 1. What was New France?<br><br>2. What was the Ohio River valley?<br><br>3. What was Fort Duquesne?<br><br>4. What was the Ohio River valley?<br><br>5. What was France? | 1. What were forts (or stockades)?<br><br>2. What were log cabins?<br><br>3. What was the Church of England? | 1. What was the Ohio River?<br><br>2. What was the Mississippi?<br><br>3. What was Lake Erie? |
| **10** | 4. What were settlers?<br><br>5. Who was Louis Montcalm?<br><br>6. Who was James Wolfe? | 6. What was Quebec?<br><br>7. What was Virginia?<br><br>8. What was Fort Pitt?<br><br>9. What was Kentucky?<br><br>10. What is Europe? | 4. What was the Albany Plan of Union?<br><br>5. What was Spain?<br><br>6. What was a powder horn? | 4. What is the Hudson?<br><br>5. What was the Mississippi River?<br><br>6. What was the Mohawk? |
| **15** | 7. Who was William Pitt?<br><br>8. Who were the Iroquois?<br><br>9. Who was Louis XIV?<br><br>10. What are allies? | 11. What were the Appalachian Mountains?<br><br>12. What was Louisbourg?<br><br>13. What is Pittsburgh?<br><br>14. What was Spain?<br><br>15. What was Florida? | 7. What was Roman Catholic?<br><br>8. What was a road?<br><br>9. What was a cliff? | 7. What is the St. Lawrence?<br><br>8. What is Lake Ontario?<br><br>9. What are the Allegheny and the Monongahela?<br><br>10. What was the Allegheny? |
| **20** | 11. Who was Benjamin Franklin?<br><br>12. Who was Louis Montcalm?<br><br>13. Who was Robert Dinwiddie?<br><br>14. Who were the Hurons and Algonquins? | 16. What were the Plains of Abraham?<br><br>17. What was Deerfield?<br><br>18. What was Spain?<br><br>19. What is the island of Great Britain?<br><br>20. What was Fort Necessity? | 10. What was the Peace of Paris?<br><br>11. What were forts?<br><br>12. What was the Seven Years' War? | 11. What is Lake Ontario?<br><br>12. What was the St. Lawrence?<br><br>13. What was Lake Champlain? |

# 7  Steps Leading to Revolution

| | Makers of the Revolution | Important Locations | Acts and Laws | Ingredients of the Revolution |
|---|---|---|---|---|
| **5** | 1. Who was Paul Revere? <br><br> 2. Who was George III? <br><br> 3. Who were the Sons of Liberty? <br><br> 4. What was a redcoat (or a lobsterback)? <br><br> 5. What were the Minutemen? | 1. What was Boston? <br><br> 2. What was Philadelphia? <br><br> 3. What was Massachusetts? <br><br> 4. What was Boston? | 1. What was the Stamp Act? <br><br> 2. What were the Townshend Acts? <br><br> 3. What was the Proclamation of 1763? <br><br> 4. What is repeal? | 1. What were smuggled goods? <br><br> 2. What were Committees of Correspondence? <br><br> 3. What was "No taxation without representation"? <br><br> 4. What was a direct tax? <br><br> 5. What was the French and Indian War? |
| **10** | 6. Who was Patrick Henry? <br><br> 7. Who was Thomas Gage? <br><br> 8. Who was Samuel Adams? <br><br> 9. Who were the Continentals? <br><br> 10. Who were Tories? | 5. What was New York? <br><br> 6. What were the Appalachians? <br><br> 7. What were Lexington and Concord? <br><br> 8. What was Massachusetts? | 5. What was the Declaratory Act? <br><br> 6. What were the Navigation Acts? <br><br> 7. What was the Proclamation of 1763? <br><br> 8. What were the Navigation Acts? | 6. What is representative government? <br><br> 7. What was a boycott? <br><br> 8. What was the First Continental Congress? <br><br> 9. What were muskets? <br><br> 10. What were imports? <br><br> 11. What were mobs? |
| **15** | 11. Who was Samuel Adams? <br><br> 12. Who was Pontiac? <br><br> 13. Who was John Adams? <br><br> 14. Who was Samuel Prescott? <br><br> 15. Who was Patrick Henry? | 9. What were American homes? <br><br> 10. What was Massachusetts? <br><br> 11. What was Virginia? <br><br> 12. What was Concord? | 9. What were the Intolerable Acts? <br><br> 10. What was the Declaration of Rights? <br><br> 11. What was the Quebec Act? | 12. What was the House of Burgesses? <br><br> 13. What was Parliament? <br><br> 14. What was a duty? <br><br> 15. What was a petition? <br><br> 16. What was tarring and feathering? <br><br> 17. What was Pontiac's War? |
| **20** | 16. Who was George Grenville? <br><br> 17. Who was James Otis? <br><br> 18. Who was Crispus Attucks? <br><br> 19. Who was John Hancock? | 13. What was New York? <br><br> 14. What was Massachusetts? <br><br> 15. What was the Charles River? <br><br> 16. What was Boston? | 12. What was the Quartering Act? <br><br> 13. What were the Virginia Resolutions? <br><br> 14. What was the First Continental Congress? | 18. What were enumerated articles? <br><br> 19. What were Writs of Assistance? <br><br> 20. What was tea? <br><br> 21. What was the British East India Company? <br><br> 22. What is a monopoly? <br><br> 23. What is tyranny? |

# 8  The American Revolution

| | People of the Revolution | Important Locations | Important Elements | Famous Quotations |
|---|---|---|---|---|
| **5** | 1. Who was George Washington?<br>2. Who was George III?<br>3. Who were the Hessians?<br>4. Who were the Loyalists (or Tories)?<br>5. Who was Benedict Arnold?<br>6. Who was John Paul Jones?<br>7. Who was Francis Marion?<br>8. Who was Cornwallis? | 1. What was the Atlantic Ocean?<br>2. What was France?<br>3. What was Valley Forge?<br>4. What was Mount Vernon?<br>5. What was Paris?<br>6. What was Pennsylvania? | 1. What was the Declaration of Independence?<br>2. What was Parliament?<br>3. What was independence?<br>4. What is a white flag? | 1. What did Patrick Henry say?<br>2. What did Benjamin Franklin say?<br>3. What did Nathan Hale say?<br>4. What did John Paul Jones say? |
| **10** | 9. Who was Barry St. Leger?<br>10. Who was Baron von Steuben?<br>11. Who was John Burgoyne?<br>12. Who was Ethan Allen?<br>13. Who was Nathanael Greene?<br>14. Who was George Rogers Clark?<br>15. Who was Marquis de Lafayette? | 7. What was Saratoga?<br>8. What were Montreal and Quebec?<br>9. What was the Delaware River?<br>10. What was the Mississippi?<br>11. What was Chesapeake Bay?<br>12. What were the Great Lakes? | 5. What was the Second Continental Congress?<br>6. What was *Common Sense*?<br>7. What were earthworks?<br>8. What was the *Bonhomme Richard*? | 5. What did Thomas Paine say?<br>6. Who was George Washington?<br>7. What did Thomas Jefferson write?<br>8. What did Patrick Henry say? |
| **15** | 16. Who was Benjamin Franklin?<br>17. Who was Thomas Jefferson?<br>18. Who was Thomas Paine?<br>19. Who was William Prescott?<br>20. Who was William Howe?<br>21. Who was Richard Henry Lee? | 13. What was Chesapeake Bay?<br>14. What was Vincennes?<br>15. What was Virginia?<br>16. What was Germany?<br>17. What was Philadelphia?<br>18. What was Breed's Hill? | 9. What were tar and feathers?<br>10. What was a blockade?<br>11. What was the *Serapis*?<br>12. What were cannons?<br>13. What were privateers?<br>14. What was a continental? | 9. What did Benjamin Franklin say?<br>10. What did Thomas Jefferson say?<br>11. What did William Prescott say?<br>12. What did Nathanael Greene write? |
| **20** | 22. Who was Richard Montgomery?<br>23. Who was Henry Clinton?<br>24. Who were Pulaski and Kosciuszko?<br>25. Who was John Burgoyne?<br>26. Who was Molly Pitcher?<br>27. Who was Louis XVI? | 19. What was Boston?<br>20. What were Ticonderoga and Crown Point?<br>21. What was Florida?<br>22. What was Lake Champlain?<br>23. What was the Hudson?<br>24. What was the Gulf of St. Lawrence? | 15. What was *Poor Richard's Almanack*?<br>16. What was the Olive Branch Petition? | 13. What did George Washington tell his troops?<br>14. What did George Washington tell Congress?<br>15. What did Benjamin Franklin say?<br>16. What did Richard Henry Lee say? |

# 9  A New Government

| | Government of the People | Important Locations | The Trappings of Government | The Government's Ideas and Powers |
|---|---|---|---|---|
| 5 | 1. Who was Benjamin Franklin?<br>2. Who was George Washington?<br>3. Who was Thomas Jefferson?<br>4. Who was Alexander Hamilton?<br>5. Who was Thomas Jefferson?<br>6. Who was John Adams?<br>7. Who was John Marshall? | 1. What is the Atlantic Ocean?<br>2. What were rivers?<br>3. What was Mount Vernon?<br>4. What was Philadelphia?<br>5. What was Virginia? | 1. What were the Articles of Confederation?<br>2. What was the Northwest Ordinance?<br>3. What is Congress?<br>4. What is the Bill of Rights?<br>5. What is the Cabinet?<br>6. What is District of Columbia?<br>7. What was the Whiskey Tax? | 1. What are amendments?<br>2. What is the system of checks and balances?<br>3. What is a veto?<br>4. What was the lack of a strong central government? |
| 10 | 8. Who was Henry Knox?<br>9. Who was John Adams?<br>10. What are members of the House of Representatives?<br>11. Who was James Madison?<br>12. Who was Thomas Jefferson?<br>13. What are senators? | 6. What was New Hampshire?<br>7. What was Delaware?<br>8. What was France?<br>9. What was New Orleans?<br>10. What is the Gulf of Mexico?<br>11. What is the Ohio? | 8. What was the Federalist party?<br>9. What was the Democratic-Republican party?<br>10. What was nine?<br>11. What were legislatures?<br>12. What were the *Federalist Papers*? | 5. What was taxing power?<br>6. What was the Virginia Plan?<br>7. What was ratification?<br>8. What is a compromise? |
| 15 | 14. Who was John Adams?<br>15. Who was Patrick Henry?<br>16. Who was Thomas Jefferson?<br>17. Who was Daniel Shays? | 12. What is the Potomac?<br>13. What is the Potomac?<br>14. What was the Northwest Territory?<br>15. What was Virginia?<br>16. What is the Savannah?<br>17. What was Maryland? | 13. What was a section?<br>14. What is the House of Representatives?<br>15. What is the executive branch?<br>16. What is the Constitution?<br>17. What is the Senate?<br>18. What was all the states? | 9. What is a tariff?<br>10. What was neutrality?<br>11. What was the New Jersey Plan?<br>12. What is a confederation?<br>13. What were the Articles of Confederation? |
| 20 | 18. Who was James Madison?<br>19. Who were John Jay, James Madison, and Alexander Hamilton?<br>20. Who was Roger Sherman?<br>21. Who was Thomas Pinckney?<br>22. Who was (citizen) Edmond Genet? | 18. What were Rhode Island and North Carolina?<br>19. What was Annapolis, Maryland?<br>20. What was Spain?<br>21. What was Rhode Island?<br>22. What was Pennsylvania? | 19. What was the judicial branch?<br>20. What was the Jay Treaty?<br>21. What was the Central Congress?<br>22. What was a township?<br>23. What were public schools?<br>24. What are legislative, executive, and judicial? | 14. What is the right of deposit?<br>15. What is a republic?<br>16. What is a federal form of government? |

## 10 | Testing the New Government

| | Important People | Important Locations | Affairs of the New Government | Concepts Important to the New Government |
|---|---|---|---|---|
| 5 | 1. Who was Alexander Hamilton? <br><br> 2. Who was Thomas Jefferson? <br><br> 3. Who was George Washington? <br><br> 4. Who was John Jay? <br><br> 5. Who was John Adams? | 1. What was the Potomac? <br><br> 2. What were Virginia and Maryland? <br><br> 3. What was Mount Vernon? <br><br> 4. What was Washington? | 1. What was the Federalist party? <br><br> 2. What is the Bill of Rights? <br><br> 3. What is the Bill of Rights? <br><br> 4. What is the House of Representatives? | 1. What is a candidate? <br><br> 2. What is debt? <br><br> 3. What is nomination? |
| 10 | 6. Who was George Washington? <br><br> 7. Who was John Adams? <br><br> 8. Who was Aaron Burr? <br><br> 9. Who were X, Y, and Z? <br><br> 10. Who was Alexander Hamilton? | 5. What was Philadelphia? <br><br> 6. What was the District of Columbia? | 5. What was money? <br><br> 6. What was the federal government? <br><br> 7. What were bonds? <br><br> 8. What was whiskey? | 4. What is inauguration? <br><br> 5. What was impressing? <br><br> 6. What are taxes? |
| 15 | 11. Who was John Jay? <br><br> 12. Who was George Washington? <br><br> 13. Who was Alexander Hamilton? <br><br> 14. Who was Thomas Jefferson? | 7. What was Pennsylvania? <br><br> 8. What was the mint? <br><br> 9. What was France? | 9. What was the National Bank? <br><br> 10. What was the Assumption Plan? <br><br> 11. What was Jay's Treaty? <br><br> 12. What was the Convention of 1800? | 7. What is neutrality? <br><br> 8. What were Federalists? <br><br> 9. What is an excise tax? |
| 20 | 15. Who was (citizen) Edmond Genet? <br><br> 16. Who were Alexander Hamilton and Thomas Jefferson? <br><br> 17. Who was Thomas Jefferson? <br><br> 18. Who was Alexander Hamilton? | 10. What was Great Britain? <br><br> 11. What was France? <br><br> 12. What is the White House? | 13. What was the Alien Act? <br><br> 14. What were the Alien and Sedition Acts? <br><br> 15. What was the Democratic-Republican party? | 10. What is a bond? <br><br> 11. What is a tariff? <br><br> 12. What is sedition? <br><br> 13. What is a political party? |

# 11 | Politics

| | People in Politics | Places of Political Importance | Political Concepts | Political Things |
|---|---|---|---|---|
| 5 | 1. What is the vice president? <br><br> 2. What is a governor? <br><br> 3. What is a mayor? <br><br> 4. What are officials? <br><br> 5. What is the president? | 1. What is Washington, D.C.? <br><br> 2. What is the Post Office? <br><br> 3. What is the District of Columbia? | 1. What is a majority? <br><br> 2. What is protest? <br><br> 3. What is a minority? <br><br> 4. What is propaganda? <br><br> 5. What is amnesty? <br><br> 6. What is veto power? | 1. What is the Constitution? <br><br> 2. What are jury members? <br><br> 3. What is a demonstration? <br><br> 4. What is the federal government? <br><br> 5. What is a law? |
| 10 | 6. What is a candidate? <br><br> 7. What is the vice president? <br><br> 8. What is the Chief Justice? <br><br> 9. What is a voter? <br><br> 10. What is a dictator? | 4. What is the Potomac? <br><br> 5. What is the Senate? <br><br> 6. What is the House of Representatives? | 7. What is nationalism? <br> 8. What is the system of checks and balances? <br> 9. What is enforce? <br> 10. What is a compromise? <br> 11. What are civil rights? <br> 12. What is elect? | 6. What is the executive branch? <br><br> 7. What is the Bill of Rights? <br><br> 8. What is Congress? <br><br> 9. What is a treaty? <br><br> 10. What is Congress? <br><br> 11. What is a petition? |
| 15 | 11. What is a council? <br><br> 12. What is a king or queen (or monarch)? <br><br> 13. What are representatives? <br><br> 14. What is a political scientist? <br><br> 15. What is the president? | 7. What were Maryland and Virginia? <br><br> 8. What is the Capitol? <br><br> 9. What is the White House? | 13. What is a democracy? <br><br> 14. What is an impeachment? <br><br> 15. What is divine right? <br><br> 16. What is absolute power? <br><br> 17. What is repeal? <br><br> 18. What is prohibit? | 12. What is a court? <br><br> 13. What are amendments? <br><br> 14. What is the Bill of Rights? <br><br> 15. What are qualifications? <br><br> 16. What is a term? |
| 20 | 16. Who was Gerald Ford? <br> 17. What are senators? <br> 18. What were suffragists? <br> 19. What is a lobbyist? <br> 20. What is the secretary of state? <br> 21. What is speaker of the House? | 10. What is the House of Representatives? <br><br> 11. What is Blair House? <br><br> 12. What is Congress? | 19. What is communism? <br><br> 20. What is suffrage? <br><br> 21. What is ratify? <br><br> 22. What is integration? <br><br> 23. What is intervention? | 17. What is a poll? <br> 18. What is a convention? <br> 19. What is the Eighteenth Amendment? <br> 20. What is the Supreme Court? <br> 21. What is a senator? |

# 12 | The War of 1812 and an Expanding Nation

|  | Important People | Sites of Action | War on the Water | Events and Policies |
|---|---|---|---|---|
| 5 | 1. Who was Thomas Jefferson? <br> 2. Who were Lewis and Clark? <br> 3. What were the War Hawks? <br> 4. Who was Francis Scott Key? <br> 5. Who was Sacajawea? <br> 6. What were pioneers? | 1. What was France? <br> 2. What was Washington, D.C.? <br> 3. What was the Mississippi River? <br> 4. What is the Gulf of Mexico? <br> 5. What was Canada? <br> 6. What was Toronto? | 1. What was the *Constitution?* <br> 2. What was Great Britain? <br> 3. What were the Great Lakes? | 1. What was the Monroe Doctrine? <br> 2. What was the War of 1812? |
| 10 | 7. Who was Daniel Boone? <br> 8. Who was Napoleon? <br> 9. Who was James Madison? <br> 10. Who was Tecumseh? <br> 11. Who were Henry Clay and John C. Calhoun? <br> 12. Who was Oliver Hazard Perry? | 7. What was Fort McHenry? <br> 8. What was Spain? <br> 9. What was St. Louis? <br> 10. What is Pike's Peak? <br> 11. What was the Great American Desert? <br> 12. What was Lake Erie? | 4. What was impressing? <br> 5. What is freedom of the seas? | 3. What were England and France? <br> 4. What was the spoils system? |
| 15 | 13. Who was Andrew Jackson? <br> 14. Who was James Monroe? <br> 15. Who was James Madison? <br> 16. Who was Zebulon Pike? <br> 17. Who was John Jacob Astor? <br> 18. Who was Jedediah Smith? | 13. What was the Cumberland Gap? <br> 14. What was Fort McHenry? <br> 15. What was Lake Champlain? <br> 16. What was New England? <br> 17. What was Chicago? <br> 18. What was Fort Niagara? | 6. What were American ships? <br> 7. What was the *Chesapeake?* <br> 8. What were prize ships? | 5. What was neutrality? <br> 6. What is the frontier? |
| 20 | 19. Who was William Henry Harrison? <br> 20. Who were James Monroe and Robert Livingston? <br> 21. Who was Dolley Madison? <br> 22. Who was Andrew Jackson? <br> 23. Who was Thomas Macdonough? <br> 24. Who was Henry Clay? | 19. What was Kentucky? <br> 20. What was Florida? <br> 21. What was South Carolina? <br> 22. What was Ghent, Belgium? <br> 23. What was the Columbia? | 9. What was a blockade? <br> 10. What was the Embargo Act? | 7. What was the Federalist party? <br> 8. What was the Treaty of Ghent? <br> 9. What was a hurricane? |

## 13 The Mexican War and Westward Expansion

|  | Names Americans Knew | Places Americans Went | Westward Expansion | Political Events and Ideas |
|---|---|---|---|---|
| 5 | 1. Who was James K. Polk?<br>2. Who was Zachary Taylor?<br>3. What were the forty-niners?<br>4. Who was Stephen Austin?<br>5. Who was Winfield Scott?<br>6. Who was James Marshall? | 1. What was Mexico?<br>2. What was the Alamo?<br>3. What was Texas?<br>4. What was Oregon Territory?<br>5. What was Texas?<br>6. What is the Pacific Ocean? | 1. What was a railroad?<br>2. What was gold?<br>3. What was the Oregon Trail? | 1. What was slavery?<br>2. What was a republic?<br>3. What was "Remember the Alamo"? |
| 10 | 7. Who was Brigham Young?<br>8. Who was Joseph Smith?<br>9. Who was Santa Anna?<br>10. Who was Sam Houston?<br>11. Who was James Gadsden?<br>12. Who was John Sutter? | 7. What was San Antonio?<br>8. What was Utah?<br>9. What is the Great Salt Lake?<br>10. What was the Rio Grande?<br>11. What was the Gulf of Mexico?<br>12. What was California? | 4. What were wagon trains?<br>5. What was the Conestoga wagon?<br>6. What were land grants? | 4. What was (Roman) Catholicism?<br>5. What is a white flag?<br>6. What was the Compromise of 1850? |
| 15 | 13. Who was Santa Anna?<br>14. Who was Stephen Kearney?<br>15. Who was Winfield Scott?<br>16. Who was John C. Fremont?<br>17. Who was Zachary Taylor?<br>18. Who was John Slidell? | 13. What was San Jacinto?<br>14. What was Veracruz?<br>15. What was Spain?<br>16. What was the Battle of Buena Vista?<br>17. What was Oregon?<br>18. What was the Nueces? | 7. What was manifest destiny?<br>8. What is irrigation?<br>9. What was the Gadsden Purchase? | 7. What was the Bear Flag revolt?<br>8. What was the Treaty of Guadalupe Hidalgo?<br>9. What was a ban on Texas settlements? |
| 20 | 19. Who was William Barret Travis?<br>20. Who was Moses Austin?<br>21. Who was Nicholas Trist?<br>22. Who were Jim Bowie and Davy Crockett?<br>23. What was the Donner party?<br>24. Who were Marcus and Narcissa Whitman? | 19. What was the Gila?<br>20. What were the Colorado and Brazos?<br>21. What was Mexico City?<br>22. What was Guadalupe Hidalgo?<br>23. What was the Platte (or the Missouri) River?<br>24. What was the Snake? | 10. What were clipper ships?<br>11. What is the Bowie knife?<br>12. What was St. Louis? | 10. What was the Wilmot Proviso?<br>11. What was the Whig party?<br>12. What was popular sovereignty?<br>13. What was the Mexican Cession? |

## 14 Science and Inventions

| | Inventors and Inventions | Important Locations | Transportation and Communication | Industrial Growth |
|---|---|---|---|---|
| 5 | 1. Who was Eli Whitney?<br>2. Who was James Watt?<br>3. Who was Robert Fulton?<br>4. Who was Samuel Slater?<br>5. Who was Eli Whitney? | 1. What was a city?<br>2. What were slums (or ghettos)?<br>3. What was the South?<br>4. What was the Erie Canal? | 1. What was the *Clermont?*<br>2. What is Morse code?<br>3. What was the stagecoach?<br>4. What was the Pony Express?<br>5. What were flatboats? | 1. What is a factory?<br>2. What were the New England textile mills?<br>3. What were slaves? |
| 10 | 6. Who was Samuel Colt?<br>7. Who was Cyrus McCormick?<br>8. Who was Donald McKay?<br>9. Who was Isaac Singer?<br>10. Who was De Witt Clinton? | 5. What was Great Britain?<br>6. What were rivers?<br>7. What was California?<br>8. What was the Mohawk? | 6. What was the Erie Canal?<br>7. What was a toll?<br>8. What was *Tom Thumb?*<br>9. What were Conestoga wagons?<br>10. What was a river pilot? | 4. What was the Industrial Revolution?<br>5. What are machine tools?<br>6. What is a combine? |
| 15 | 11. Who was Peter Cooper?<br>12. Who was Samuel F.B. Morse?<br>13. Who was Daniel Boone?<br>14. Who was Cyrus W. Field?<br>15. Who was John Butterfield?<br>16. Who was Elias Howe? | 9. What was St. Joseph?<br>10. What was New England?<br>11. What was the Cumberland Gap?<br>12. What were Washington, D.C., and Baltimore, Maryland? | 11. What was Clinton's Big Ditch (or Clinton's Folly)?<br>12. What was a towpath?<br>13. What was the telegraph?<br>14. What were locks?<br>15. What was the *Savannah?* | 7. What is specialization?<br>8. What was mass production?<br>9. What were immigrants? |
| 20 | 17. Who was John Deere?<br>18. Who was Charles Goodyear?<br>19. Who was Cornelius Vanderbilt?<br>20. Who was Robert Gray?<br>21. Who was Francis Cabot Lowell? | 13. What was Rhode Island?<br>14. What was Albany?<br>15. What were Albany and Buffalo?<br>16. What was the Hudson? | 16. What was a cowcatcher?<br>17. What was the Atlantic cable?<br>18. What was the *Flying Cloud?*<br>19. What was mail delivery?<br>20. What were clipper ships? | 10. What were interchangeable parts?<br>11. What was the War of 1812?<br>12. What is technology? |

## 15  Prelude to the Civil War

| | Important People | Important Locations | Background Factors | Background Ideas |
|---|---|---|---|---|
| **5** | 1. Who was Eli Whitney?<br>2. Who was Henry Clay?<br>3. Who was John C. Calhoun?<br>4. What were abolitionists?<br>5. Who was Abraham Lincoln?<br>6. Who was John Brown? | 1. What was the North?<br>2. What was Missouri?<br>3. What was South Carolina?<br>4. What was Fort Sumter?<br>5. What was Richmond, Virginia? | 1. What was cotton?<br>2. What was slavery?<br>3. What were plantations?<br>4. What was *Uncle Tom's Cabin*?<br>5. What was the Confederate States of America | 1. What is compromise?<br>2. What is abolition?<br>3. What was a free state?<br>4. What is a civil war? |
| **10** | 7. Who was Abraham Lincoln?<br>8. Who was Jefferson Davis?<br>9. Who was Harriet Beecher Stowe?<br>10. Who was Henry Clay?<br>11. Who was Harriet Tubman?<br>12. Who was Dred Scott? | 6. What was the North Star?<br>7. What was Canada?<br>8. What was Maine?<br>9. What was Kentucky?<br>10. What was Liberia? | 6. What was a lawyer?<br>7. What was a tariff?<br>8. What was the *Liberator*?<br>9. What was the Compromise of 1850?<br>10. What were slave codes? | 5. What is states' rights?<br>6. What was secession?<br>7. What was the Great Compromiser?<br>8. What was Bleeding Kansas? |
| **15** | 13. Who was Abraham Lincoln?<br>14. Who were Daniel Webster and Robert Hayne?<br>15. Who was Frederick Douglass?<br>16. Who was Stephen A. Douglas?<br>17. Who was John Brown?<br>18. What was Moses? | 11. What were the Western Territories?<br>12. What was the Senate?<br>13. What was California?<br>14. What was South Carolina?<br>15. What was Harpers Ferry? | 11. What was the Kansas-Nebraska Act?<br>12. What was the Republican party?<br>13. What was the Underground Railroad?<br>14. What was *The North Star*?<br>15. What was the American Colonization Society? | 9. What was the Little Giant?<br>10. What was a fugitive?<br>11. What is inauguration?<br>12. What was the Doctrine of Nullification? |
| **20** | 19. Who was Pierre Beauregard?<br>20. Who was John C. Fremont?<br>21. Who was Roger B. Taney?<br>22. Who was Nat Turner?<br>23. Who was John C. Breckenridge? | 16. What was Kansas?<br>17. What was South Carolina?<br>18. What were stations?<br>19. What was Mississippi?<br>20. What was Lawrence?<br>21. What was Pottawatomie Creek?<br>22. What was Shawnee Mission?<br>23. What was Montgomery, Alabama? | 16. What was the Tariff of Abominations?<br>17. What was the Wilmot Proviso?<br>18. What was the *Dred Scott* case? | 13. What was popular sovereignty?<br>14. What was property?<br>15. What is a debate? |

## 16  The Civil War

|  | Americans at War | Sites of Warfare | Factors Related to the War | Terms of the War |
|---|---|---|---|---|
| 5 | 1. Who was Abraham Lincoln?<br>2. What was Honest Abe?<br>3. What were abolitionists?<br>4. Who was Robert E. Lee?<br>5. Who was Ulysses S. Grant?<br>6. Who was John Wilkes Booth? | 1. What was Appomattox Courthouse?<br>2. What was Atlanta?<br>3. What was Gettysburg?<br>4. What was the Mississippi?<br>5. What is the Gulf of Mexico?<br>6. What is the Mississippi? | 1. What was the Republican party?<br>2. What was cotton?<br>3. What was the Emancipation Proclamation?<br>4. What was the North? | 1. What was secession?<br>2. What were border states?<br>3. What were blockades?<br>4. What was Reconstruction? |
| 10 | 7. Who was Jefferson Davis?<br>8. Who was Andrew Johnson?<br>9. Who was Stephen A. Douglas?<br>10. Who was George B. McClellan?<br>11. Who was Thomas Jackson?<br>12. What was Stonewall? | 7. What is the Atlantic Ocean?<br>8. What was Bull Run?<br>9. What was Antietam?<br>10. What was Montgomery, Alabama?<br>11. What was Gettysburg?<br>12. What was Vicksburg? | 5. What was West Virginia?<br>6. What was farming (or agriculture)?<br>7. What was a lawyer?<br>8. What was the Thirteenth Amendment? | 5. What is surrender?<br>6. What is defensive war?<br>7. What is offensive war?<br>8. What are regiments? |
| 15 | 13. Who was Ulysses S. Grant?<br>14. Who was William Tecumseh Sherman?<br>15. Who was John Ericsson?<br>16. Who was J.E.B. Stuart?<br>17. Who was George E. Pickett? | 13. What were Texas, Louisiana, and Arkansas?<br>14. What was Chattanooga?<br>15. What was West Virginia?<br>16. What is the Potomac? | 9. What were blockade-runners?<br>10. What was 11?<br>11. What was West Point?<br>12. What was the *Monitor*?<br>13. What was the *Merrimac* (or *Virginia*)?<br>14. What was the Gettysburg Address? | 9. What are casualties?<br>10. What are military objectives?<br>11. What was the Anaconda Plan?<br>12. What was a siege? |
| 20 | 18. Who was David G. Farragut?<br>19. Who was George B. McClellan?<br>20. Who was Edwin Stanton?<br>21. Who was William Seward?<br>22. Who was George Gordon Meade? | 17. What was Savannah?<br>18. What was Chancellorsville?<br>19. What were Missouri, Kentucky, Maryland, and Delaware?<br>20. What was Hampton Roads?<br>21. What was Bull Run? | 15. What was England or France? [Name one.]<br>16. What were its generals?<br>17. What was the Army of Northern Virginia? | 13. What is a strategy?<br>14. What is assassination?<br>15. What were mines (or torpedoes)?<br>16. What were ironclads? |

# 17 Reconstruction

| | People in Reconstruction | Reconstruction in Progress | Important Locations | Terms of Reconstruction |
|---|---|---|---|---|
| **5** | 1. What were carpetbaggers?<br><br>2. Who was John Wilkes Booth?<br><br>3. What were freedmen?<br><br>4. Who was Andrew Johnson? | 1. What was a veto?<br><br>2. What were voting and holding public office?<br><br>3. What were ghosts?<br><br>4. What was education?<br><br>5. What was Congress? | 1. What was Washington, D.C.?<br><br>2. What was the South? | 1. What was fear?<br><br>2. What was equality?<br><br>3. What are legislatures?<br><br>4. What is to ratify? |
| **10** | 5. What were scalawags?<br><br>6. What were sharecroppers?<br><br>7. Who was Ulysses S. Grant?<br><br>8. Who was Andrew Johnson? | 6. What is a secret ballot?<br>7. What was the Thirteenth Amendment?<br>8. What was the Fourteenth Amendment?<br>9. What was Reconstruction?<br>10. What was the Freedmen's Bureau?<br>11. What were black codes? | 3. What was Tennessee?<br><br>4. What was Ford's Theater?<br><br>5. What was Tennessee? | 5. What was white supremacy?<br><br>6. What are customs?<br><br>7. What is impeachment? |
| **15** | 9. Who was Clara Barton?<br><br>10. Who were the Radicals?<br><br>11. Who was Edwin Stanton?<br><br>12. What was a tenant farmer? | 12. What was the Fourteenth Amendment?<br>13. What was the Fifteenth Amendment?<br>14. What was the Ku Klux Klan?<br>15. What was the Democratic party?<br>16. What was the Tenure of Office Act?<br>17. What was the Ten Percent Plan? | 6. What were military districts?<br><br>7. What was Springfield, Illinois? | 8. What is segregation?<br><br>9. What is uneducated (or illiterate)?<br><br>10. What was military rule? |
| **20** | 13. Who was Samuel J. Tilden?<br><br>14. Who is the Supreme Court Chief Justice?<br><br>15. Who was Charles Sumner?<br><br>16. Who was Thaddeus Stevens?<br><br>17. Who was Rutherford B. Hayes? | 18. What was the Fourteenth Amendment?<br>19. What was April 1865?<br>20. What was a poll tax?<br>21. What was a literacy test?<br>22. What were Jim Crow laws? | 8. What was the Solid South?<br><br>9. What was prison? | 11. What are civil rights?<br><br>12. What is an unconstitutional law?<br><br>13. What is radical?<br><br>14. What were second-class citizens? |

# 18   Life on the Great Plains

|  | People of the Plains | Places on the Plains | Ranching and Settlement | Indian Life |
|---|---|---|---|---|
| 5 | 1. Who were Lewis and Clark?<br><br>2. What was the Pony Express?<br><br>3. What were cowboys? | 1. What is the Mississippi River?<br><br>2. What are the Rocky Mountains?<br><br>3. What was Promontory, Utah? | 1. What is grass?<br><br>2. What was the Great American Desert?<br><br>3. What was the horse?<br><br>4. What is a brand?<br><br>5. What was barbed wire? | 1. What was the buffalo?<br><br>2. What was land?<br><br>3. What was farming? |
| 10 | 4. Who were the Pawnee?<br><br>5. Who was General Custer?<br><br>6. Who were the Sioux?<br><br>7. Who was Crazy Horse? | 4. What are the Black Hills?<br><br>5. What is the Missouri?<br><br>6. What was Fort Laramie? | 6. What is a stampede?<br>7. What was five years?<br>8. What were longhorns?<br>9. What was the transcontinental railroad?<br>10. What was open range?<br>11. What was the railroad? | 4. What are nomads?<br><br>5. What was counting coup?<br><br>6. What was the iron horse?<br><br>7. What was a reservation? |
| 15 | 8. Who was Sitting Bull?<br><br>9. Who was Geronimo?<br><br>10. Who was Joseph Glidden?<br><br>11. Who was Colonel Chivington? | 7. What is Oklahoma?<br><br>8. What was Montana?<br><br>9. What were the Black Hills? | 12. What was a chuck wagon?<br>13. What was sod?<br>14. What was the Chisholm Trail?<br>15. What was a drive?<br>16. What was the Homestead Act?<br>17. What was land? | 8. What was pemmican?<br><br>9. What was Custer's Last Stand?<br><br>10. What was a travois?<br><br>11. What was sign language? |
| 20 | 12. Who was Black Kettle?<br><br>13. What were homesteaders?<br><br>14. Who were the Nez Percé? | 10. What is the Gulf of Mexico?<br><br>11. What were stockyards?<br><br>12. What was Chicago? | 18. What was a windmill?<br><br>19. What was Oklahoma?<br><br>20. What was the Kansas-Nebraska Act?<br><br>21. What were grasshoppers? | 12. What was the Sioux War?<br><br>13. What was Sand Creek?<br><br>14. What was the Trail of Tears?<br><br>15. What was the Bureau of Indian Affairs? |

## 19 | New Inventions and Transportation

| | Builders and Doers | Important Locations | Inventions and Discoveries | Terms of Progress |
|---|---|---|---|---|
| 5 | 1. Who was Andrew Carnegie?<br>2. Who was John D. Rockefeller?<br>3. Who was Thomas Alva Edison?<br>4. Who was Henry Ford?<br>5. What are immigrants?<br>6. Who was Alexander Graham Bell? | 1. What are seaports?<br>2. What is Pittsburgh?<br>3. What were cities?<br>4. What was Pennsylvania?<br>5. What was Detroit? | 1. What was the Model T?<br>2. What was a wireless?<br>3. What was the *Spirit of St. Louis?*<br>4. What was barbed wire? | 1. What are interchangeable (or standardized) parts?<br>2. What was an assembly line?<br>3. What is petroleum?<br>4. What is a monopoly? |
| 10 | 7. Who was Charles Eastman?<br>8. Who were the Chinese?<br>9. Who was Henry Bessemer?<br>10. Who was George Pullman?<br>11. Who was Eli Whitney?<br>12. Who was Charles Lindbergh? | 6. What was Paris?<br>7. What was Kitty Hawk, North Carolina?<br>8. What was Dayton, Ohio?<br>9. What were textile mills?<br>10. What was Ogden, Utah? | 5. What was steel?<br>6. What were horseless carriages?<br>7. What was the Bessemer process?<br>8. What was Morse code? | 5. What is commerce?<br>6. What is division of labor?<br>7. What was the Industrial Revolution?<br>8. What was coke? |
| 15 | 13. Who was Thomas Watson?<br>14. Who was George Westinghouse?<br>15. Who was Cyrus W. Field?<br>16. Who was Charles Lindbergh?<br>17. Who was Samuel F.B. Morse?<br>18. Who was Orville Wright? | 11. What were factories?<br>12. What was Scotland?<br>13. What was Menlo Park, New Jersey?<br>14. What was Connecticut?<br>15. What was Pittsburgh? | 9. What was the radio?<br>10. What is a converter?<br>11. What is bauxite? | 9. What is to invest?<br>10. What is manufacturing (or mass production)?<br>11. What is technology?<br>12. What is automation? |
| 20 | 19. Who was Elisha Otis?<br>20. Who was Frank W. Woolworth?<br>21. Who was Cyrus McCormick?<br>22. What is a reformer?<br>23. Who was Jane Addams? | 16. What was Lake Superior?<br>17. What are sweatshops?<br>18. What was Hull House? | 12. What is a dynamo?<br>13. What was the typewriter?<br>14. What was a Tin Lizzie? | 13. What is installment buying?<br>14. What are land, labor, and capital?<br>15. What are chain stores?<br>16. What are tenements? |

# 20 America Becomes a World Power

| | Important Leaders | Places American Power Spread | Items and Events | Terms of Power |
|---|---|---|---|---|
| 5 | 1. Who was James Cook?<br>2. Who was Theodore Roosevelt?<br>3. Who was Woodrow Wilson?<br>4. Who was William Seward?<br>5. Who was Grover Cleveland?<br>6. Who was Theodore Roosevelt? | 1. What was Alaska?<br>2. What was Alaska?<br>3. What is Pearl Harbor?<br>4. What was Panama?<br>5. What is Hawaii?<br>6. What was Denmark?<br>7. What are the Pacific Ocean and the Atlantic Ocean (or the Caribbean Sea)?<br>8. What is the Arctic Ocean?<br>9. What was Havana? | 1. What was the *Maine*?<br>2. What was the mosquito?<br>3. What were locks?<br>4. What were missionaries? | 1. What is patriotism?<br>2. What is tyranny?<br>3. What is a peace treaty?<br>4. What is independence? |
| 10 | 7. Who was William McKinley?<br>8. Who was George Dewey?<br>9. Who was Theodore Roosevelt?<br>10. Who was Leonard Wood?<br>11. Who was Carlos Finlay?<br>12. Who was William Gorgas?<br>13. Who was John Hay? | 10. What were the Virgin Islands?<br>11. What was Russia?<br>12. What was Spain?<br>13. What is the Bering Strait?<br>14. What is Manila Bay?<br>15. What are the Philippine Islands?<br>16. What was San Juan Hill?<br>17. What is Siberia? | 5. What was gold?<br>6. What were malaria and yellow fever?<br>7. What is sugar? | 5. What are guerrillas?<br>6. What was annexation?<br>7. What were expansionists?<br>8. What is imperialism? |
| 15 | 14. Who was Matthew Perry?<br>15. Who was Robert Gray?<br>16. Who was Sanford Dole?<br>17. Who was William Randolph Hearst?<br>18. Who was William Seward?<br>19. Who was Vitus Bering? | 18. What was Nicaragua?<br>19. What was China?<br>20. What is Alaska?<br>21. What is the Far East?<br>22. What was Guantánamo Bay?<br>23. What is the Caribbean?<br>24. What was Samoa? | 8. What was the *Maine*?<br>9. Who were Polynesians?<br>10. What was the *Oregon*? | 9. What was the open-door policy?<br>10. What is an armistice?<br>11. What is a revolution?<br>12. What is reform? |
| 20 | 20. Who was Queen Liliuokalani?<br>21. Who was Emilio Aguinaldo?<br>22. Who was Walter Reed?<br>23. Who was George Goethals?<br>24. Who was Woodrow Wilson?<br>25. Who was Kamehameha I? | 25. What is Pago Pago?<br>26. What was Spain?<br>27. What was Colombia?<br>28. What were Wake and Guam?<br>29. What were Puerto Rico, Cuba, and the Philippines? | 11. What was sugar cane?<br>12. What was the Jones Act?<br>13. What was the Spanish-American War?<br>14. What was the Nobel Peace Prize? | 13. What is propaganda?<br>14. What is yellow journalism?<br>15. What was "to speak softly and carry a big stick"?<br>16. What were Progressives?<br>17. What is regulation? |

# 21 Government, Business, and Labor

| | Important Leaders | Getting Organized | Forms of Business | Regulation by Law |
|---|---|---|---|---|
| **5** | 1. Who was John D. Rockefeller?<br><br>2. Who was Samuel Gompers?<br><br>3. Who was Andrew Carnegie?<br><br>4. Who was John L. Lewis? | 1. What was the Knights of Labor?<br>2. What are labor unions?<br>3. What is a strike?<br>4. What is a contract?<br>5. What was the A.F.L. (American Federation of Labor)?<br>6. What was a brotherhood? | 1. What is a monopoly?<br><br>2. What is profit?<br><br>3. What is competition?<br><br>4. What is a partnership?<br><br>5. What are employees?<br><br>6. What are demands? | 1. What was the Civil Service?<br><br>2. What was the National Labor Relations Act?<br><br>3. What was the Pure Food and Drug Act? |
| **10** | 5. Who was Theodore Roosevelt?<br><br>6. Who was William McKinley?<br><br>7. Who was John L. Lewis?<br><br>8. Who was Oliver Kelly? | 7. What is a craft union?<br>8. What is collective bargaining?<br>9. What are scabs?<br>10. What was the Grange?<br>11. What is an industrial union? | 7. What was pooling?<br>8. What is interstate commerce?<br>9. What are dividends?<br>10. What are shares of stock?<br>11. What were rebates?<br>12. What are stockholders (or shareholders)? | 4. What was the Sherman Anti-Trust Act?<br><br>5. What was the Interstate Commerce Act?<br><br>6. What was the Interstate Commerce Commission? |
| **15** | 9. Who was Jay Gould?<br><br>10. Who was Theodore Roosevelt?<br><br>11. Who was William Howard Taft?<br><br>12. Who was J.P. Morgan?<br><br>13. Who was Uriah Stephens? | 12. What is a cooling-off period?<br><br>13. What is a lockout?<br><br>14. What are injunctions?<br><br>15. What was Chicago?<br><br>16. What was a closed shop? | 13. What are proprietors?<br><br>14. What is a corporation?<br><br>15. What is a board of directors?<br><br>16. What is capital?<br><br>17. What is a trust?<br><br>18. What is a merger? | 7. What was the Morrill Act?<br><br>8. What was the Fair Labor Standards Act?<br><br>9. What was the Clayton Anti-Trust Act? |
| **20** | 14. Who was Terence Powderly?<br><br>15. Who were Robert Taft and Fred Hartley?<br><br>16. Who was Eugene V. Debs?<br><br>17. Who was Upton Sinclair? | 17. What was a yellow-dog contract?<br>18. What was the Haymarket Square riot?<br>19. What is the Brotherhood of Locomotive Engineers?<br>20. What was the International Workers of the World? | 19. What is a conglomerate?<br><br>20. What was a holding company?<br><br>21. What is limited liability?<br><br>22. What is free enterprise? | 10. What was the National Labor Relations Act?<br><br>11. What was the Taft-Hartley Act?<br><br>12. What was the Triangle Shirtwaist Company fire? |

## 22 | World War I

| | Important People | Sites of War | War Words and Phrases | War on the Water |
|---|---|---|---|---|
| **5** | 1. Who was Archduke Ferdinand?<br>2. Who was Kaiser Wilhelm II?<br>3. Who was Woodrow Wilson?<br>4. Who was John J. Pershing?<br>5. Who was Woodrow Wilson?<br>6. Who was Woodrow Wilson? | 1. What was Austria-Hungary?<br>2. What was Versailles?<br>3. What was Belgium?<br>4. What was Serbia?<br>5. What was Italy?<br>6. What was the Western Front? | 1. What were trenches?<br>2. What were tanks?<br>3. What were grenades?<br>4. What was imperialism?<br>5. What was the Treaty of Versailles?<br>6. What was the Triple Alliance?<br>7. What was the Triple Entente? | 1. What is the English Channel?<br>2. What is Gibraltar?<br>3. What was the Atlantic Ocean?<br>4. What were submarines?<br>5. What is the Mediterranean Sea?<br>6. What was a blockade? |
| **10** | 7. Who was David Lloyd George?<br>8. Who was Georges Clemenceau?<br>9. Who was Woodrow Wilson?<br>10. Who was Alfred Zimmerman?<br>11. Who was Baron Manfred von Richthofen?<br>12. Who was Ferdinand Foch? | 7. What was Great Britain?<br>8. What was the Eastern Front?<br>9. What was Great Britain?<br>10. What was Russia?<br>11. What was Belgium?<br>12. What was the United States? | 8. What were the Central Powers?<br>9. What is nationalism?<br>10. What were the Fourteen Points?<br>11. What is armistice?<br>12. What was the airplane?<br>13. What was the draft?<br>14. What were the Allies? | 7. What is the Suez Canal?<br>8. What is the Black Sea?<br>9. What is Gibraltar?<br>10. What is the North Sea?<br>11. What is the Red Sea?<br>12. What was the Baltic Sea? |
| **15** | 13. Who was Nicholas II?<br>14. Who was Woodrow Wilson?<br>15. Who was Vittorio Orlando?<br>16. Who was Prince Otto von Bismarck?<br>17. Who was Colonel House? | 13. What was Germany?<br>14. What was Russia?<br>15. What was the Balkan Peninsula?<br>16. What was Germany?<br>17. What was Russia?<br>18. What was Czechoslovakia? | 15. What was doughboy?<br>16. What is an arms race?<br>17. What was the American Expeditionary Force?<br>18. What was no-man's-land?<br>19. What was a "scrap of paper"?<br>20. What was neutrality?<br>21. What is isolationism? | 13. What were the Bosporus and the Dardanelles?<br>14. What is the Seine?<br>15. What is the Arctic Ocean?<br>16. What was the North Sea?<br>17. What is the Adriatic Sea?<br>18. What is the North Sea? |
| **20** | 18. Who was Nicholas II?<br>19. Who was Schlieffen?<br>20. Who was Pancho Villa?<br>21. Who was Gavrilo Princip?<br>22. Who was Eddie Rickenbacker? | 19. What was Germany?<br>20. What was France?<br>21. What was the Second Battle of the Marne?<br>22. What was Saint Mihiel?<br>23. What is Argonne? | 22. What is a balance of power?<br>23. What is self-determination?<br>24. What was the League of Nations?<br>25. What is propaganda?<br>26. What were reparations? | 19. What was unrestricted submarine warfare?<br>20. What was the convoy system?<br>21. What was the *Lusitania*?<br>22. What was the *Sussex*?<br>23. What was Jutland? |

# 23 | Between the World Wars

|  | Important People | Domestic Boom and Bust | Sites of Action | International Events |
|---|---|---|---|---|
| **5** | 1. Who was Warren G. Harding?<br><br>2. Who was Calvin Coolidge?<br><br>3. Who was Herbert Hoover?<br><br>4. Who was Warren G. Harding? | 1. What was the Social Security Act?<br><br>2. What was the New Deal?<br><br>3. What was the Civilian Conservation Corps?<br><br>4. What was the Republican party?<br><br>5. What is unemployment? | 1. What was Teapot Dome?<br><br>2. What was Washington, D.C.?<br><br>3. What is the stock exchange? | 1. What was the League of Nations?<br><br>2. What was the League of Nations?<br><br>3. What was the Senate? |
| **10** | 5. Who was Franklin Roosevelt?<br><br>6. Who was Calvin Coolidge?<br><br>7. Who was Henry Cabot Lodge?<br><br>8. Who was Frank B. Kellogg? | 6. What were the Roaring Twenties?<br><br>7. What was the Eighteenth Amendment?<br><br>8. What was the (Great) Depression?<br><br>9. What was the stock market?<br><br>10. What was the Nineteenth Amendment? | 4. What were the United States, Japan, France, Italy, and Great Britain? [Name three.]<br><br>5. What was Elk Hills?<br><br>6. What was the Tennessee? | 4. What was the World Court?<br><br>5. What was the Washington Conference?<br><br>6. What were isolationists? |
| **15** | 9. Who was Warren G. Harding?<br><br>10. Who was Franklin Roosevelt?<br><br>11. Who was Franklin Roosevelt?<br><br>12. Who was Elihu Root? | 11. What is a depression?<br><br>12. What were banks?<br><br>13. What was the Public Works Administration?<br><br>14. What was the Tennessee Valley Authority? | 7. What are the Great Plains?<br><br>8. What was Japan?<br><br>9. What were Hoovervilles? | 7. What was "make it safe for democracy"?<br><br>8. What was the quota system? |
| **20** | 13. Who was Charles Evans Hughes?<br><br>14. Who was Albert B. Fall?<br><br>15. Who was Eleanor Roosevelt? | 15. What was the Works Progress Administration?<br><br>16. What was the Agricultural Adjustment Administration?<br><br>17. What were fireside chats?<br><br>18. What is a bureaucracy? | 10. What was Geneva, Switzerland?<br><br>11. What was Geneva, Switzerland?<br><br>12. What was The Hague? | 9. What was the International Labor Organization?<br><br>10. What was the Kellogg-Briand Pact? |

# 24 Economics

| | Important People | Places in Our Economy | Things in the U.S. Economy | Economic Principles |
|---|---|---|---|---|
| **5** | 1. What is an economist? <br> 2. What are employers? <br> 3. What is a stockholder (or shareholder)? <br> 4. What is a trader? <br> 5. What are employees? | 1. What is a factory? <br> 2. What are banks? <br> 3. What is a sweatshop? | 1. What are goods? <br> 2. What are wages? <br> 3. What is a loan? <br> 4. What is money? <br> 5. What is profit? <br> 6. What are taxes? <br> 7. What is price? | 1. What is division of labor? <br> 2. What is barter or trade? <br> 3. What is recycle? <br> 4. What is a boycott? <br> 5. What is inflation? <br> 6. What is mass production? |
| **10** | 6. What is a debtor? <br> 7. What is a specialist? <br> 8. What is an investor? <br> 9. What is a consumer? | 4. What is an assembly line? <br> 5. What is Wall Street? | 8. What is an advertisement? <br> 9. What is collateral? <br> 10. What is principal? <br> 11. What are services? <br> 12. What is capital? <br> 13. What is interest? <br> 14. What is a market? | 7. What is scarcity? <br> 8. What is capitalism? <br> 9. What is investment? <br> 10. What are luxuries? <br> 11. What is prosperity? |
| **15** | 10. What is a stockbroker? <br> 11. What is a producer? <br> 12. What is a proprietor? <br> 13. What is a creditor? | 6. What is the New York Stock Exchange (or NASDAQ)? <br> 7. What is a refinery? | 15. What is income tax? <br> 16. What is a bond? <br> 17. What is a check? <br> 18. What are dividends? <br> 19. What is net income? | 12. What is supply? <br> 13. What is shift work? <br> 14. What is interdependence? <br> 15. What is a recession? <br> 16. What is deflation? <br> 17. What is deficit spending? |
| **20** | 14. What is a wholesaler? <br> 15. What is an entrepreneur? <br> 16. What is a retailer? <br> 17. What is the management? | 8. What are exchanges? <br> 9. What is a retail store? <br> 10. What is a wholesale store? | 20. What is a medium of exchange? <br> 21. What are corporations? <br> 22. What is a budget? <br> 23. What are consumer goods? <br> 24. What is the gross national product (gross domestic product)? <br> 25. What is overhead? | 18. What is free enterprise? <br> 19. What is market research? <br> 20. What is a depression? <br> 21. What is demand? <br> 22. What is installment buying? |

## 25 | America at Home, 1920–1940

| | Law and Crime | Entertainment | Slang Comes of Age | The Sports World |
|---|---|---|---|---|
| **5** | 1. Who was Al Capone? <br><br> 2. What was the Eighteenth Amendment? <br><br> 3. Who were Sacco and Vanzetti? <br><br> 4. What was the Scopes (or monkey) trial? | 1. What was *The Jazz Singer*? <br> 2. Who was Louis Armstrong? <br> 3. What was KDKA? <br> 4. Who was Will Rogers? <br> 5. What were crossword puzzles? <br> 6. What was *Gone with the Wind*? <br> 7. What was flagpole-sitting? | 1. What is a young girl of the 1920s? <br> 2. What is an important person? <br> 3. What is a date with an unknown person? <br> 4. What is to murder? <br> 5. What is an infatuation with another person? <br> 6. What is a chorus girl or dancer? | 1. Who was Babe Ruth? <br><br> 2. Who was Jack Dempsey? <br><br> 3. Who was Floyd Collins? <br><br> 4. What is baseball's Hall of Fame? |
| **10** | 5. What was the FBI? <br><br> 6. Who was Charles Lindbergh? <br><br> 7. What were bootleggers? <br><br> 8. What was a flask? | 8. Who was Sinclair Lewis? <br> 9. What was *The Grapes of Wrath*? <br> 10. Who were the Marx Brothers? <br> 11. Who was Rudolph Valentino? <br> 12. Who was George Gershwin? <br> 13. What was the Charleston? | 7. What is an old car? <br> 8. What is to vomit? <br> 9. What are FBI (government) men? <br> 10. What is tough? <br> 11. What is a person who uses charm to get money? <br> 12. What is a person who is blamed? | 5. What is Yankee Stadium? <br><br> 6. Who was Gene Tunney? <br><br> 7. Who was Jim Thorpe? <br><br> 8. Who was Man o' War? |
| **15** | 9. What were speakeasies? <br><br> 10. What was bathtub gin? <br><br> 11. Who was J. Edgar Hoover? <br><br> 12. What was the St. Valentine's Day massacre? | 14. Who was Charlie Chaplin? <br> 15. What was marathon dancing? <br> 16. What was "War of the Worlds"? <br> 17. What were fireside chats? <br> 18. Who was Fred Astaire? <br> 19. Who was Shirley Temple? <br> 20. Who was F. Scott Fitzgerald? <br> 21. What was the Castle Walk? | 13. What is anything super or wonderful? <br> 14. What is bad, contemptible? <br> 15. What is to arrest? <br> 16. What is to leave in a hurry? <br> 17. What is a hired gunman? <br> 18. What is having an elegant appearance? | 9. Who was Ty Cobb? <br><br> 10. Who was Bill Tilden? <br><br> 11. Who was Bobby Jones? <br><br> 12. Who was Gertrude Ederle? |
| **20** | 13. Who were Loeb and Leopold? <br><br> 14. Who was John Dillinger? <br><br> 15. Who was Pretty Boy Floyd? <br><br> 16. Who was Ma Barker? | 22. Who was Lon Chaney? <br> 23. Who was Mickey Rooney? <br> 24. Who was Eugene O'Neill? <br> 25. Who was H. L. Mencken? <br> 26. Who was Charles Lindbergh? | 19. What is something genuine? <br> 20. What is a female's leg? <br> 21. What is anything wonderful? <br> 22. What is a superb person or thing? <br> 23. What is popular music that grew out of the heritage of African Americans? | 13. Who was Johnny Weissmuller? <br><br> 14. Who was Knute Rockne? <br><br> 15. Who was Red Grange? <br><br> 16. Who was Jesse Owens? |

## 26 | The World Heads Toward War

| | The Leaders | The Places | Things People Talked About | Ideas That Led to War |
|---|---|---|---|---|
| 5 | 1. Who was Franklin Roosevelt?<br><br>2. Who was Neville Chamberlain?<br><br>3. Who was Frank B. Kellogg?<br><br>4. Who was Adolf Hitler? | 1. What was Italy?<br><br>2. What was Germany?<br><br>3. What was the Rhineland?<br><br>4. What was the United States?<br><br>5. What was Munich? | 1. What was the Maginot Line?<br><br>2. What was the Versailles Treaty?<br><br>3. What were the Atlantic and Pacific oceans?<br><br>4. What was Il Duce? | 1. What was isolationism?<br><br>2. What is a dictator?<br><br>3. What is neutrality?<br><br>4. What are alliances? |
| 10 | 5. Who was Benito Mussolini?<br><br>6. Who was Joseph Stalin?<br><br>7. Who was Francisco Franco?<br><br>8. Who was Neville Chamberlain?<br><br>9. Who was Henry L. Stimson? | 6. What was Berlin?<br><br>7. What was Rome?<br><br>8. What was Manchuria?<br><br>9. What was Ethiopia?<br><br>10. What was Japan? | 5. Who were the Jews?<br><br>6. What were Nazis?<br><br>7. What was Manchukuo?<br><br>8. What was a reduction of arms? | 5. What is totalitarianism?<br><br>6. What is appeasement?<br><br>7. What is nationalism? |
| 15 | 10. Who was Hirohito?<br><br>11. Who was Adolf Hitler?<br><br>12. Who was Cordell Hull?<br><br>13. Who was Edouard Daladier?<br><br>14. Who was Chiang Kai-shek? | 11. What was China?<br><br>12. What was Canada?<br><br>13. What was Japan?<br><br>14. What was the Soviet Union? | 9. What was the League of Nations?<br><br>10. What was the (Great) Depression?<br><br>11. What were Neutrality Acts?<br><br>12. Who were storm troopers? | 8. What were reparations?<br><br>9. What is aggression?<br><br>10. What was the Axis? |
| 20 | 15. Who was Haile Selassie?<br><br>16. Who was Albert Einstein?<br><br>17. Who was Enrico Fermi?<br><br>18. Who was Haile Selassie? | 15. What was Austria?<br><br>16. What was Spain?<br><br>17. What was Austria?<br><br>18. What was Finland?<br><br>19. What was the Sudetenland? | 13. What was the *Panay*?<br><br>14. What was the Johnson Debt Default Act?<br><br>15. What was the Siegfried Line?<br><br>16. What was the Manhattan Project?<br><br>17. What was rationing? | 11. What is pacifism?<br><br>12. What is a police state?<br><br>13. What is the draft? |

# 27 World War II

| | Civilian Leaders | Military Leaders | War in Europe and Africa | War in the Pacific |
|---|---|---|---|---|
| **5** | 1. Who was Adolf Hitler?<br>2. Who was Benito Mussolini?<br>3. Who was Hideki Tojo?<br>4. Who was Winston Churchill?<br>5. Who was Joseph Stalin?<br>6. Who was Harry Truman? | 1. Who was Dwight Eisenhower?<br><br>2. Who was Franklin Roosevelt?<br><br>3. Who was Douglas MacArthur? | 1. What was Poland?<br>2. What was the English Channel?<br>3. What was the Suez Canal?<br>4. What was the Soviet Union?<br>5. What was the North Sea?<br>6. What was the Black Sea? | 1. What was Japan?<br>2. What was Japan?<br>3. What is the Pacific Ocean?<br>4. What was Pearl Harbor?<br>5. What was China?<br>6. What were the Philippines? |
| **10** | 7. Who was Franklin D. Roosevelt?<br>8. Who was Franklin D. Roosevelt?<br>9. Who was Adolf Hitler?<br>10. Who was Harry Truman?<br>11. Who was Marshall Pétain?<br>12. What were women? | 4. Who was Dwight Eisenhower?<br><br>5. Who was Douglas MacArthur?<br><br>6. Who was Erwin Rommel?<br><br>7. Who was Chester Nimitz? | 7. What was Finland?<br>8. What was Dunkirk?<br>9. What was France?<br>10. What was Vichy?<br>11. What was Russia (or the Soviet Union)?<br>12. What was France?<br>13. What was France? | 7. What is Manila?<br>8. What was Hiroshima?<br>9. What were aircraft carriers?<br>10. What was the *Missouri?*<br>11. What was Nagasaki?<br>12. What was Guadalcanal? |
| **15** | 13. Who was Albert Einstein?<br>14. Who was Eleanor Roosevelt?<br>15. Who was George VI?<br>16. Who was Clement Attlee?<br>17. Who was Mussolini?<br>18. Who was Joseph Goebbels? | 8. Who was Claire Chennault?<br><br>9. Who was Erwin Rommel?<br><br>10. Who was Sir Bernard Montgomery? | 14. What was El Alamein?<br>15. What is France?<br>16. What were Sicily and Italy?<br>17. What is Egypt?<br>18. What was Yalta?<br>19. What was Albania?<br>20. What was Compiègne? | 13. What were Iwo Jima and Okinawa?<br>14. What was Singapore?<br>15. What was Bataan, the Philippines?<br>16. What were the Aleutians?<br>17. What was Corregidor? |
| **20** | 19. Who was Heinrich Himmler?<br>20. Who was Heinrich Himmler?<br>21. Who was Chiang Kai-shek?<br>22. Who was Charles de Gaulle?<br>23. Who was Thomas E. Dewey? | 11. Who were Chester Nimitz and William Halsey?<br><br>12. Who was Hermann Goering?<br><br>13. Who was George C. Marshall? | 21. What was the Atlantic Ocean?<br>22. What was the Adriatic Sea?<br>23. What was Normandy?<br>24. What was radar?<br>25. What was Stalingrad? | 18. What were the Philippine Islands?<br>19. What is Oahu?<br>20. What was the Coral Sea?<br>21. What is the Coral Sea?<br>22. What is the Sea of Japan? |

## 28 The Postwar Years

| | People in the News | Postwar Terms | Laws and Organizations | Places in the News |
|---|---|---|---|---|
| **5** | 1. Who was Harry Truman?<br><br>2. Who was Harry Truman?<br><br>3. What is a veteran?<br><br>4. Who was Thomas E. Dewey? | 1. What was a GI?<br><br>2. What is a strike?<br><br>3. What are human rights?<br><br>4. What is communism? | 1. What was the Department of Defense?<br><br>2. What was the United Nations?<br><br>3. What is the Security Council?<br><br>4. What is the World Health Organization? | 1. What was Berlin?<br><br>2. What is the United States?<br><br>3. What was Germany? |
| **10** | 5. Who was Trygve Lie?<br><br>6. Who was Dean Acheson?<br><br>7. Who was George C. Marshall?<br><br>8. Who was Douglas MacArthur? | 5. What is demobilize?<br><br>6. What is inflation?<br><br>7. What was the Cold War?<br><br>8. What were displaced persons? | 5. What is the Secretariat?<br><br>6. What is the General Assembly?<br><br>7. What was the GI Bill of Rights?<br><br>8. What was the Taft-Hartley Act? | 4. What was the Soviet Union?<br><br>5. What is Washington, D.C.?<br><br>6. What was Berlin? |
| **15** | 9. Who was Dag Hammarskjöld?<br><br>10. Who was Anne Frank?<br><br>11. What were communists?<br><br>12. Who was Harry Truman? | 9. What are underdeveloped nations?<br><br>10. What is the secretary general?<br><br>11. What is an injunction?<br><br>12. What was a cooling-off period? | 9. What was the Communist party?<br><br>10. What is the International Court of Justice?<br><br>11. What was the Atomic Energy Act?<br><br>12. What is the Economic and Social Council? | 7. What is The Hague, Netherlands?<br><br>8. What was Nuremberg?<br><br>9. What are China, France, Great Britain, the United States, and the Soviet Union?<br><br>10. What was San Francisco? |
| **20** | 13. What were communist groups?<br><br>14. Who was Andrei Gromyko?<br><br>15. What were war criminals? | 13. What were Dixiecrats?<br><br>14. What are fissionable materials?<br><br>15. What was containment?<br><br>16. What is an airlift? | 13. What was the Twenty-second Amendment?<br><br>14. What was the Marshall Plan?<br><br>15. What was the Atomic Energy Commission?<br><br>16. What was the Office of Scientific Research and Development? | 11. What was West Germany?<br><br>12. What was Dunbarton Oaks?<br><br>13. What was the Soviet Union? |

## 29 The Korean War

|  | War Leaders | Sites of Warfare | Important Terms | Participants in the War |
|---|---|---|---|---|
| 5 | 1. Who was Harry Truman?<br><br>2. Who was Chiang Kai-shek?<br><br>3. Who was Joseph Stalin?<br><br>4. Who was Dwight Eisenhower? | 1. What was Korea?<br><br>2. What was Japan?<br><br>3. What is North Korea?<br><br>4. What is the Far East?<br><br>5. What is Seoul? | 1. What is a protest?<br><br>2. What is a delegate?<br><br>3. What is a blockade?<br><br>4. What is a stalemate? | 1. What were the prisoners? |
| 10 | 5. Who was Douglas MacArthur?<br><br>6. Who was Mao Tse-tung?<br><br>7. Who was Syngman Rhee? | 6. What was Panmunjom?<br><br>7. What is the Yalu?<br><br>8. What was Japan?<br><br>9. What was the Soviet Union?<br><br>10. What was the Republic of Korea? | 5. What is a veto?<br><br>6. What is communism?<br><br>7. What is containment?<br><br>8. What is an aggressor? | 2. What were helicopters?<br><br>3. What were MIG-15 airplanes? |
| 15 | 8. Who was Harry Truman?<br><br>9. Who was Chiang Kai-shek?<br><br>10. Who was Douglas MacArthur? | 11. What was the United States?<br><br>12. What was Wake Island?<br><br>13. What was Inchon?<br><br>14. What is the Sea of Japan?<br><br>15. What is the Korean Strait? | 9. What was brainwashing?<br><br>10. What is limited war?<br><br>11. What is repatriation? | 4. What was the Security Council?<br><br>5. What was the Seventh Fleet? |
| 20 | 11. Who was Jacob Malik?<br><br>12. Who were Harry Truman and Douglas MacArthur?<br><br>13. Who was Matthew B. Ridgway? | 16. What was the Soviet Union?<br><br>17. What was China?<br><br>18. What was Pusan?<br><br>19. What is the 38th parallel? | 12. What is a demilitarized zone?<br><br>13. What is an armistice?<br><br>14. What is a police action? | 6. What were volunteers? |

# 30 The Cold War

| | Important Leaders | Places People Talked About | Events, Groups, and Objects of Conflict | Terms of Conflict |
|---|---|---|---|---|
| 5 | 1. Who was Joseph Stalin?<br><br>2. Who was Fidel Castro?<br><br>3. Who was John F. Kennedy?<br><br>4. Who was Mao Tse-tung? | 1. What was Moscow?<br>2. What is Cuba?<br>3. What is the Middle East?<br>4. What is the Mediterranean Sea?<br>5. What is the Strait of Gibraltar?<br>6. What was France?<br>7. What is Egypt? | 1. What was World War II?<br><br>2. What was the Communist party?<br><br>3. What was the Berlin Wall?<br><br>4. What was the United Nations? | 1. What is a cold war?<br><br>2. What are alliances?<br><br>3. What is a dictator? |
| 10 | 5. Who was Lyndon Johnson?<br><br>6. Who was Winston Churchill?<br><br>7. Who was Dwight Eisenhower?<br><br>8. Who was Nikita Khrushchev? | 8. What were Greece and Turkey?<br><br>9. What was Israel?<br><br>10. What was Berlin?<br><br>11. What was Berlin?<br><br>12. What was Berlin? | 5. What was sugar?<br><br>6. What was the Berlin Airlift?<br><br>7. What was the Communist party?<br><br>8. What were missiles?<br><br>9. What was the Suez Canal? | 4. What is a blockade?<br><br>5. What was the Iron Curtain?<br><br>6. What is the policy of containment? |
| 15 | 9. Who was Joseph Stalin?<br><br>10. Who was Lyndon Johnson?<br><br>11. Who was Henry Kissinger?<br><br>12. Who was President Kennedy? | 13. What is Siberia?<br>14. What was Finland?<br>15. What were Turkey and Greece?<br>16. What was East Germany?<br>17. What were France, Great Britain, the Soviet Union, and the United States? | 10. What was *Sputnik*?<br><br>11. What was the North Atlantic Treaty Organization (or NATO)?<br><br>12. What was the May Day parade?<br><br>13. What was the General Assembly? | 7. What were satellites?<br><br>8. What was the Cuban Missile Crisis?<br><br>9. What was a nuclear threat? |
| 20 | 13. Who was Lenin?<br><br>14. Who was Batista?<br><br>15. Who were the Freedom Fighters?<br><br>16. Who was Richard Nixon? | 18. What was Indochina?<br><br>19. What was Yugoslavia?<br><br>20. What is the Gulf of Suez?<br><br>21. What was Formosa?<br><br>22. What was Hungary? | 14. What is a soviet?<br><br>15. What was the Warsaw Pact?<br><br>16. What was the Organization of American States?<br><br>17. What was NASA (National Aeronautics and Space Administration)? | 10. What is totalitarian?<br><br>11. What is guerrilla warfare?<br><br>12. What is subjugation? |

# 31 Prejudice

| | People and Prejudice | Laws and Groups | Terms of Prejudice | Places Prejudice Was Felt |
|---|---|---|---|---|
| 5 | 1. What are immigrants?<br>2. What were slaves?<br>3. Who was Martin Luther King, Jr.?<br>4. Who was John Brown?<br>5. Who was Harriet Beecher Stowe?<br>6. Who was Martin Luther King, Jr.? | 1. What was the Ku Klux Klan?<br>2. What was the Black Panthers?<br>3. What is the National Organization for Women (NOW)?<br>4. What is the Bureau of Indian Affairs?<br>5. What was Red Power? | 1. What is race?<br>2. What are civil rights?<br>3. What is a majority?<br>4. What was a sit-in?<br>5. What is prejudice?<br>6. What is a minority? | 1. What were reservations?<br>2. What is the Southwest?<br>3. What is a tenement? |
| 10 | 7. Who were the Irish?<br>8. What were indentured servants?<br>9. What were abolitionists?<br>10. Who were Elizabeth Cady Stanton and Susan B. Anthony? [Name one.] | 6. What was the Southern Christian Leadership Conference (SCLC)?<br>7. What was the National Urban League?<br>8. What was the Emancipation Proclamation?<br>9. What was the Underground Railroad?<br>10. What is the National Association for the Advancement of Colored People (NAACP)? | 7. What is segregation?<br>8. What is protesting?<br>9. What was busing?<br>10. What was a boycott? | 4. What are sweatshops?<br>5. What is a ghetto?<br>6. What was Ireland? |
| 15 | 11. Who was Rosa Parks?<br>12. Who were the Nisei?<br>13. Who was Betty Friedan?<br>14. What was Chicano?<br>15. Who was Ralph Abernathy?<br>16. Who was Harriet Tubman? | 11. What was the Twenty-fourth Amendment?<br>12. What was the Thirteenth Amendment?<br>13. What was the Nineteenth Amendment?<br>14. What was the Know-Nothing party?<br>15. What was the *Dred Scott* decision? | 11. What are stereotypes?<br>12. What is integration?<br>13. What is a melting pot?<br>14. What is discrimination? | 7. What was Montgomery, Alabama?<br>8. What was Alcatraz?<br>9. What is a *barrio*? |
| 20 | 17. Who was Booker T. Washington?<br>18. Who was Nat Turner?<br>19. Who was César Chavez?<br>20. Who was William Lloyd Garrison?<br>21. Who was Frederick Douglass? | 16. What were Jim Crow laws?<br>17. What is the National Association for the Advancement of Colored People?<br>18. What was the Fourteenth Amendment?<br>19. What was the Civil Rights Act?<br>20. What was the Fair Housing Act?<br>21. What is (Roman) Catholicism? | 15. What is a second-class citizen?<br>16. What is assimilation?<br>17. What is alien?<br>18. What is suffrage? | 10. What were relocation centers?<br>11. What was the back of the bus?<br>12. What are migrant workers? |

## 32 The Cities

| | City Dwellers | Places People Live and Work | Cities and Governments | Getting In and Out of the City |
|---|---|---|---|---|
| 5 | 1. What are landlords?<br><br>2. What are immigrants?<br><br>3. What is a sociologist? | 1. What is urban?<br><br>2. What is a suburb?<br><br>3. What are slums?<br><br>4. What is a ghetto?<br><br>5. What were farms?<br><br>6. What are residential areas? | 1. What are taxes?<br><br>2. What are reformers?<br><br>3. What was New York City? | 1. What is asphalt?<br><br>2. What is transportation?<br><br>3. What is concrete? |
| 10 | 4. What is a city manager?<br><br>5. Who was Franklin Roosevelt?<br><br>6. Who was Lyndon Johnson? | 7. What is an industrial park?<br>8. What is the inner city?<br>9. What is a metropolitan area?<br>10. What are shopping centers?<br>11. What is a mall?<br>12. What is a skyscraper? | 4. What is Central Park?<br><br>5. What was the Clean Air Act?<br><br>6. What was Haight-Ashbury? | 4. What is mass transit?<br><br>5. What was the Interstate Highway System?<br><br>6. What is out-migration? |
| 15 | 7. Who was William Marcy Tweed?<br><br>8. Who was Jane Addams?<br><br>9. Who was Fiorello La Guardia? | 13. What is urban renewal?<br>14. What were cities?<br>15. What are tenements?<br>16. What is a commercial area?<br>17. What are green belts (or parks)?<br>18. What is a duplex? | 7. What was Los Angeles?<br><br>8. What was Boston?<br><br>9. What was the Economic Opportunity Act? | 7. What is in-migration?<br><br>8. What were streetcars? |
| 20 | 10. Who was Frank Lloyd Wright?<br><br>11. Who was Buckminster Fuller? | 19. What are condominiums?<br><br>20. What is a megalopolis?<br><br>21. What is a site?<br><br>22. What is *barrio*? | 10. What was the Department of Housing and Urban Development (HUD)?<br><br>11. What was the Federal Housing Authority?<br><br>12. What is a building code? | 9. What is a subway?<br><br>10. What is a commuter train? |

## 33 | How Well Do You Know the Sixties?

| | Politics | Cultural and Public Events | Race Relations | Law and Crime |
|---|---|---|---|---|
| 5 | 1. Who was John F. Kennedy?<br>2. What was Cuba?<br>3. Who was Fidel Castro?<br>4. What was Panama?<br>5. What was Hanoi?<br>6. What was Paris?<br>7. Who was Richard Nixon? | 1. Who was John Glenn?<br>2. What was Mercury?<br>3. Who was Neil Armstrong?<br>4. Who were the Beatles?<br>5. What were miniskirts? | 1. What were sit-ins?<br>2. Who was Martin Luther King, Jr.?<br>3. Who was Edward Brooke?<br>4. Who was César Chavez?<br>5. What was the Civil Rights Act of 1964? | 1. What was to pray?<br>2. Who was John F. Kennedy?<br>3. Who was Robert F. Kennedy?<br>4. What is marijuana? |
| 10 | 8. What was the Peace Corps?<br>9. What was Cuba?<br>10. Who was John F. Kennedy?<br>11. Who was Nikita Krushchev? | 6. Who was Sean Connery?<br>7. Who was Muhammad Ali?<br>8. What was *Laugh-In*?<br>9. What was *Hair*?<br>10. Who was Alan Shepard? | 6. Who was Martin Luther King, Jr.?<br>7. Who was Eldridge Cleaver?<br>8. What was Watts?<br>9. What was the Civil Rights Act?<br>10. Who was James Meredith? | 5. What is assassination?<br>6. Who was Edward M. Kennedy?<br>7. Who was James Earl Ray?<br>8. What was counsel (or a lawyer)? |
| 15 | 12. What was underground?<br>13. What was the Tonkin Resolution?<br>14. What was the Vietnam War?<br>15. What was the Nuclear Test Ban Treaty?<br>16. What was Medicare? | 11. What was *Silent Spring*?<br>12. What was Woodstock?<br>13. What was the *Saturday Evening Post*?<br>14. Who were Chet Huntley and David Brinkley?<br>15. What were communes? | 11. Who was Thurgood Marshall?<br>12. Who was Malcolm X?<br>13. Who was Shirley Chisholm?<br>14. Who was Stokely Carmichael? | 9. What was Dallas?<br>10. What was the Warren Commission investigation?<br>11. What is LSD?<br>12. Who was Billie Sol Estes? |
| 20 | 17. What was the Berlin Wall?<br>18. What was Cambodia?<br>19. What was the Bay of Pigs invasion?<br>20. What was reconnaissance (or spying)?<br>21. What was Laos?<br>22. What was the U.S.S. *Pueblo*? | 16. Who was Twiggy?<br>17. Who was Andy Warhol?<br>18. What was the Great Society?<br>19. What is inflation?<br>20. What was National Organization for Women (NOW)? | 15. What were Newark and Detroit?<br>16. Who was Adam Clayton Powell?<br>17. What was Washington, D.C.?<br>18. What were the Black Muslims? | 13. Who was Lee Harvey Oswald?<br>14. Who was Jack Ruby?<br>15. What was Memphis?<br>16. Who was Sirhan Sirhan? |

# 34 The Environment

| | People and Places | Farming and the Soil | Environmental Terms | Climate and Atmosphere |
|---|---|---|---|---|
| 5 | 1. What is population?<br><br>2. What is a chemist?<br><br>3. What is a desert?<br><br>4. What are the Great Lakes? | 1. What is irrigation?<br><br>2. What is to cultivate?<br><br>3. What is crop rotation?<br><br>4. What is a windbreak? | 1. What is scarce?<br>2. What is (the purpose of) conservation?<br>3. What is extinction?<br>4. What is pollution?<br>5. What is to recycle?<br>6. What is the energy crisis?<br>7. What are pesticides?<br>8. What are endangered species? | 1. What is climate?<br><br>2. What is precipitation?<br><br>3. What is a drought?<br><br>4. What is fog (or vapor)? |
| 10 | 5. What is a factory?<br><br>6. What are the Great Plains?<br><br>7. What was the Dust Bowl?<br><br>8. What is population density? | 5. What is contour plowing?<br><br>6. What is fallow land?<br><br>7. What is erosion?<br><br>8. What is a herbicide? | 9. What is hazmat?<br>10. What is decomposition?<br>11. What is adaptation?<br>12. What is interdependence?<br>13. What is algae?<br>14. What is sediment? | 5. What is smog?<br><br>6. What is atmosphere?<br><br>7. What is carbon dioxide?<br><br>8. What is wind power? |
| 15 | 9. What is a conservationist?<br><br>10. What is a meteorologist?<br><br>11. What is migration? | 9. What is intensive farming?<br><br>10. What was sod?<br><br>11. What are genetically engineered crops? | 15. What is Earth Day?<br>16. What is a watershed?<br>17. What is open space?<br>18. What is clear-cutting?<br>19. What is a subsystem?<br>20. What is a greenbelt? | 9. What is acid rain?<br>10. What is the ozone layer?<br>11. What is global warming?<br>12. What is solar power?<br>13. What is the Amazon River basin (or Brazil)? |
| 20 | 12. What is the Environmental Protection Agency (EPA)?<br><br>13. What was Lake Erie?<br><br>14. Who was Rachel Carson? | 12. What are soil salts?<br><br>13. What is organic matter? | 21. What are hazardous waste sites?<br>22. What is an ecosystem?<br>23. What is the biosphere?<br>24. What is a resource?<br>25. What are waste materials?<br>26. What is technology? | 14. What is a temperature inversion?<br><br>15. What is Indonesia?<br><br>16. What are emissions? |

## 35  Women in American History

| | Well-Known Women | Women's Work | Places and Policies | Terms Involving Women |
|---|---|---|---|---|
| 5 | 1. Who was Amelia Earhart?<br>2. Who was Helen Keller?<br>3. Who was Billie Jean King?<br>4. Who was Sacajawea?<br>5. Who was Margaret Chase Smith?<br>6. Who was Harriet Tubman? | 1. What was a governess?<br>2. What is a midwife?<br>3. What was teaching?<br>4. What was nursing the sick and wounded?<br>5. What was the Supreme Court? | 1. What was Jamestown, Virginia?<br>2. What was the home?<br>3. What was the Equal Rights Amendment?<br>4. What was her seat on the bus? | 1. What is a widow?<br>2. What was a dowry? |
| 10 | 7. Who was Anne Hutchinson?<br>8. Who was Susan B. Anthony?<br>9. Who was Carry Nation?<br>10. Who was Eleanor Roosevelt?<br>11. Who was Babe Didrikson Zaharias?<br>12. Who was Harriet Beecher Stowe? | 6. What was Hull House?<br>7. What was the American Red Cross?<br>8. What was anthropology?<br>9. What was missionary work? | 5. What was the Nineteenth Amendment?<br>6. What was the West? | 3. What were WACs?<br>4. What were WAFs?<br>5. What is the weaker sex?<br>6. What is suffrage? |
| 15 | 13. Who was Shirley Chisholm?<br>14. Who was Sandra Day O'Connor?<br>15. Who was Rachel Carson?<br>16. Who was Janet Reno?<br>17. Who was Madeleine Albright? | 10. What was secretary of labor?<br>11. What was novel-writing?<br>12. What were prisons (or insane asylums)?<br>13. What was Confederate spy? | 7. What was Chicago?<br>8. What was Wyoming? | 7. What is the Pill?<br>8. What was women's liberation?<br>9. What is temperance? |
| 20 | 18. Who was Elizabeth Cady Stanton?<br>19. Who was Amelia Bloomer?<br>20. Who was Sojourner Truth?<br>21. What was Rosie the Riveter?<br>22. Who was Sally Ride?<br>23. Who was Phillis Wheatley? | 14. What were suffragettes?<br>15. What was the Women's Christian Temperance Union?<br>16. What was president of the United States?<br>17. What was to become a doctor? | 9. What was Ohio?<br>10. What was New York?<br>11. What is *Justice*? | 10. What was voting?<br>11. What was property?<br>12. What were corsets? |

## 36 The Space Age

| | Those Who Dared | Scenes of Action | Space-age Vocabulary | Modern Hardware |
|---|---|---|---|---|
| 5 | 1. What are astronauts?<br><br>2. Who were Neil Armstrong and Edwin Aldrin?<br><br>3. Who was John Glenn? | 1. What was the moon?<br><br>2. What was the Soviet Union?<br><br>3. What is a pad?<br><br>4. What is Pluto?<br><br>5. What was a solar system? | 1. What is impact?<br>2. What is launching?<br>3. What is recovery?<br>4. What is reentry?<br>5. What is tracking?<br>6. What is weightlessness?<br>7. What is a countdown? | 1. What was Mercury?<br>2. What is a satellite?<br>3. What are Russia and the United States?<br>4. What are space shuttles?<br>5. What is a heat shield?<br>6. What were sun flares?<br>7. What was *Gemini*? |
| 10 | 4. Who was Sally Ride?<br><br>5. What was *Apollo 13*?<br><br>6. Who was John Glenn? | 6. What was *Mir*?<br><br>7. What is an orbit?<br><br>8. What is Florida?<br><br>9. What is Houston, Texas?<br><br>10. What was the Soviet Union? | 8. What is splashdown?<br><br>9. What is ignition?<br><br>10. What is liftoff?<br><br>11. What were rocks?<br><br>12. What is a flight path?<br><br>13. What is a hold? | 8. What was *Apollo*?<br>9. What was *Voyager*?<br>10. What is a probe?<br>11. What was *Sputnik I*?<br>12. What was *Telstar*?<br>13. What was *Apollo I*?<br>14. What was the Hubble Telescope? |
| 15 | 7. Who was Dwight Eisenhower?<br><br>8. Who was Yuri Gagarin?<br><br>9. Who was Robert Goddard?<br><br>10. Who were Grissom, White, and Chaffee? [Name one.] | 11. What were the United States and the Soviet Union?<br><br>12. What is Venus?<br><br>13. What was ice?<br><br>14. What is Mars?<br><br>15. What was the Sea of Tranquillity? | 14. What is docking?<br>15. What is scrub?<br>16. What is a soft landing?<br>17. What is the National Aeronautics and Space Administration?<br>18. What is escape velocity?<br>19. What is Mach 1?<br>20. What is ejection? | 15. What was Venus?<br><br>16. What is a missile shield?<br><br>17. What was Mars?<br><br>18. What was *Skylab*?<br><br>19. What was *Viking*?<br><br>20. What was *Columbia*?<br><br>21. What was *Explorer I*? |
| 20 | 11. Who was Christa McAuliffe?<br><br>12. What is space?<br><br>13. What is a space shuttle?<br><br>14. What is a space tourist? | 16. What was *Challenger*?<br><br>17. What was Cape Kennedy?<br><br>18. What is a meteor shower?<br><br>19. What was Australia?<br><br>20. What was the Outer Space Treaty? | 21. What is centrifugal force?<br><br>22. What is separation?<br><br>23. What is an encounter?<br><br>24. What is a launch window?<br><br>25. What is solar wind? | 22. What is the life-support system?<br><br>23. What was the lunar rover?<br><br>24. What was Mars?<br><br>25. What was *Pathfinder*?<br><br>26. What was *Genesis*? |

## 37 Energy

| | Energy Sources | Resource Sites | Oil | Electricity and Mining |
|---|---|---|---|---|
| **5** | 1. What was wood?<br><br>2. What was the whale?<br><br>3. What is the sun?<br><br>4. What is the tide? | 1. What is the Gulf of Mexico?<br><br>2. What is Niagara Falls?<br><br>3. What is the United States?<br><br>4. What was Alaska? | 1. What is petroleum?<br><br>2. What are supertankers?<br><br>3. What is gasoline?<br><br>4. What is OPEC (Organization of Petroleum Exporting Countries)? | 1. What is a blackout?<br><br>2. What are solar cells?<br><br>3. What is electricity? |
| **10** | 5. What is uranium?<br><br>6. What is wind?<br><br>7. What are horses? | 5. What was the Arabian Peninsula?<br><br>6. What is Venezuela?<br><br>7. What was Mexico?<br><br>8. What is a wind farm? | 5. What is a refinery?<br><br>6. What is petroleum (oil)?<br><br>7. What is kerosene?<br><br>8. What is crude oil? | 4. What are rolling blackouts?<br><br>5. What was the Tennessee Valley Authority (TVA)?<br><br>6. What is hydroelectricity? |
| **15** | 8. What is coal?<br><br>9. What is nuclear energy?<br><br>10. What is solar energy? | 9. What is the United States?<br><br>10. What are Utah and Colorado?<br><br>11. What was Pennsylvania?<br><br>12. What was the North Sea? | 9. What is a blowout?<br><br>10. What is a pipeline?<br><br>11. What are SUVs (Sport Utility Vehicles)?<br><br>12. What is the North Slope? | 7. What is shaft mining?<br><br>8. What is strip-mining?<br><br>9. What is the Federal Power Commission? |
| **20** | 11. What is waterpower?<br><br>12. What was liquid hydrogen?<br><br>13. What is geothermal energy?<br><br>14. What was Chernobyl? | 13. What is Japan?<br><br>14. What was Colorado?<br><br>15. What is Israel? | 13. What is an offshore platform well?<br><br>14. What were the Arab nations?<br><br>15. What was Saudi Arabia?<br><br>16. What was Kuwait? | 10. What is the Hoover Dam?<br><br>11. What is open-pit mining? |

# 38 The Vietnam War

| | Important People | Places on the Map | Terms of War | Items in the News |
|---|---|---|---|---|
| 5 | 1. Who was Ho Chi Minh?<br><br>2. Who was John F. Kennedy?<br><br>3. Who was Lyndon Johnson?<br><br>4. What were doves? | 1. What was Hanoi?<br><br>2. What was Cambodia?<br><br>3. What was Hanoi?<br><br>4. What was Saigon?<br><br>5. What was Paris? | 1. What is a coup (coup d'état)?<br><br>2. What is a refugee?<br><br>3. What is a rout?<br><br>4. What is a buffer zone?<br><br>5. What is containment? | 1. Who were the Viet Cong?<br><br>2. What was to train the South Vietnamese army?<br><br>3. What was the Ho Chi Minh Trail? |
| 10 | 5. What were hawks?<br><br>6. Who was Nguyen Van Thieu?<br><br>7. Who was Harry Truman?<br><br>8. Who was Richard Nixon? | 6. What was My Lai?<br>7. What was the Mekong?<br>8. What was Saigon?<br>9. What was the Mekong River delta?<br>10. What was France?<br>11. What were China and the Soviet Union? | 6. What is a combatant?<br>7. What is draft-dodging?<br>8. What is a neutral country?<br>9. What is guerrilla warfare?<br>10. What were military advisers? | 4. What were helicopters?<br><br>5. What was the 17th parallel?<br><br>6. Who were the Buddhists? |
| 15 | 9. Who was Jimmy Carter?<br><br>10. Who were the Green Berets?<br><br>11. Who was General William Westmoreland?<br><br>12. Who was Ngo Dinh Diem? | 12. What was Geneva?<br>13. What was Washington, D.C.?<br>14. What was Phnom Penh?<br>15. What was Dien Bien Phu?<br>16. What was the Tonkin Gulf? | 11. What is limited warfare?<br><br>12. What is negotiate?<br><br>13. What is an incursion (or invasion)?<br><br>14. What was the domino theory? | 7. What was Agent Orange?<br><br>8. What was the Tonkin Resolution? |
| 20 | 13. Who was Dwight Eisenhower?<br><br>14. Who was Ngo Dinh Diem?<br><br>15. Who was William Calley? | 17. What was Cambodia?<br><br>18. What was Laos?<br><br>19. What was Indochina?<br><br>20. What was Ho Chi Minh City?<br><br>21. What is the Gulf of Tonkin? | 15. What was deferment?<br><br>16. What is escalation?<br><br>17. What is a demilitarized zone?<br><br>18. What is a noncombatant? | 9. What were the Pentagon Papers?<br><br>10. What was the *Mayaguez*? |

## 39 | America's Problems in the Middle East

| | People Involved | Problems on Land | Items in the News | Problems with Water |
|---|---|---|---|---|
| 5 | 1. Who was David Ben-Gurion?<br>2. Who was the Shah?<br>3. Who was Anwar el-Sadat?<br>4. Who was Menachem Begin?<br>5. Who was the Ayatollah Khomeini?<br>6. What are refugees?<br>7. Who are Muslims?<br>8. Who are Jews (or Israelis)? | 1. What is the Middle East?<br>2. What is Egypt?<br>3. What was Israel?<br>4. What was Jerusalem?<br>5. What is Saudi Arabia?<br>6. What is Cairo?<br>7. What was Tehran? | 1. What is a cease-fire?<br>2. What was the United Nations?<br>3. What was the Six-Day War?<br>4. What is oil?<br>5. What are hostages? | 1. What is the Suez Canal?<br>2. What is the Nile?<br>3. What was the Persian Gulf? |
| 10 | 9. What were hostages?<br>10. Who are the Israelis?<br>11. Who was Gamal Abdel Nasser?<br>12. Who was Dwight Eisenhower?<br>13. Who was King Faisal?<br>14. Who was Faruk? | 8. What is Beirut?<br>9. What was Great Britain?<br>10. What was Aswan?<br>11. What is the Sinai Peninsula?<br>12. What was the Soviet Union?<br>13. What was the Gaza Strip? | 6. What was the British Commonwealth?<br>7. What was an ultimatum?<br>8. What was the Eisenhower Doctrine?<br>9. What is the Palestine Liberation Organization (PLO)?<br>10. What were suicide bombings? | 4. What is the Mediterranean Sea?<br>5. What is the Gulf of Suez?<br>6. What is the Caspian Sea? |
| 15 | 15. Who was Golda Meir?<br>16. Who was Anwar el-Sadat?<br>17. Who was Saddam Hussein?<br>18. Who was George Herbert Walker Bush?<br>19. Who was Osama bin Laden? | 14. What was Great Britain?<br>15. What were Egypt and Syria?<br>16. What was the Soviet Union?<br>17. What was Kuwait?<br>18. What is Syria?<br>19. What is Negev?<br>20. What was France? | 11. What was the Gulf War?<br>12. What was the Palestine Liberation Organization?<br>13. What was the Yom Kippur War?<br>14. What was the Baghdad Pact?<br>15. What were the Camp David Accords? | 7. What is the Gulf of Aqaba?<br>8. What was the Jordan? |
| 20 | 20. Who were the Palestinians?<br>21. Who was Moshe Dayan?<br>22. Who was King Hussein?<br>23. Who was Arthur Balfour?<br>24. Who was Yasir Arafat?<br>25. Who was Yitzhak Rabin? | 21. What were Syria and Egypt?<br>22. What were Israel and Jordan?<br>23. What is a kibbutz?<br>24. What was Iran?<br>25. What was Lebanon? | 16. What are buffer zones?<br>17. What is fundamentalism?<br>18. What was the U.S. Embassy?<br>19. What are trade sanctions? | 9. What was the Suez Canal?<br>10. What are Iraq and Iran? |

# 40 A Time of Turmoil—The Seventies

| | People in the News | Where History Was Made | Items in the News | Law and Crime |
|---|---|---|---|---|
| **5** | 1. What were 18-year-olds?<br><br>2. Who was John Dean?<br><br>3. Who was Gerald Ford?<br><br>4. Who was Gerald Ford? | 1. What was Kent State University in Ohio?<br><br>2. What was Laos?<br><br>3. What was Hanoi?<br><br>4. What was Alabama?<br><br>5. What was Paris? | 1. What was Earth Day?<br><br>2. What was the U.S. Postal Service?<br><br>3. What was DDT?<br><br>4. What was gasoline?<br><br>5. What is a bicentennial? | 1. Who was William Calley?<br><br>2. Who was Spiro Agnew?<br><br>3. Who was Leon Jaworski?<br><br>4. Who were the Plumbers?<br><br>5. What was the House Judiciary Committee? |
| **10** | 5. Who was Richard Nixon?<br><br>6. Who was Richard Nixon?<br><br>7. Who was Martha Mitchell?<br><br>8. Who was Leonid Brezhnev? | 6. What was China?<br><br>7. What was Vietnam?<br><br>8. What was the Soviet Union?<br><br>9. What was Mexico?<br><br>10. What was Afghanistan? | 6. What was the *Mayaguez*?<br><br>7. What was the military draft?<br><br>8. What was the United Mine Workers?<br><br>9. What was the *New York Times* (or the *Washington Post*)? | 6. What is a subpoena?<br><br>7. What is a pardon?<br><br>8. Who was Bert Lance?<br><br>9. Who was John Mitchell?<br><br>10. What was the Supreme Court? |
| **15** | 9. Who was Jimmy Carter?<br><br>10. Who was the Shah of Iran?<br><br>11. Who was George Meany?<br><br>12. Who was Cyrus Vance?<br><br>13. Who was Ralph Nader? | 11. What was Three Mile Island, Pennsylvania?<br>12. What was Japan?<br>13. What was China?<br>14. What was Haiphong?<br>15. What is Moscow?<br>16. What was the MX missile system?<br>17. What was Lockheed? | 10. What was Legionnaires' disease?<br><br>11. What was the Panama Canal?<br><br>12. What is a demilitarized zone?<br><br>13. What was *Roe v. Wade*? | 11. What was Attica?<br>12. Who was John Sirica?<br>13. Who was Patricia Hearst?<br>14. Who was Charles Manson?<br>15. Who were John Ehrlichman and H.R. Haldeman? |
| **20** | 14. Who was Richard Nixon?<br><br>15. What was Pahlavi?<br><br>16. Who was J. Edgar Hoover?<br><br>17. Who was Hubert Humphrey? | 18. What was California?<br><br>19. What was Wounded Knee?<br><br>20. What was the Watergate?<br><br>21. What was Libya? | 14. What was the Strategic Arms Agreement?<br>15. What was the War Powers bill?<br>16. What was the Energy Department (or Department of Energy)?<br>17. What was OPEC (Organization of Petroleum-Exporting Countries)? | 16. What was the Central Intelligence Agency (CIA)?<br><br>17. Who was Archibald Cox?<br><br>18. Who was George Wallace?<br><br>19. Who was Daniel Ellsberg? |

# 41 The Nation in the Eighties

| | People in the News | Where History Was Made | Items in the News | The Nation's Health |
|---|---|---|---|---|
| 5 | 1. Who was Christa McAuliffe?<br>2. Who was Sally Ride?<br>3. Who was Ronald Reagan?<br>4. Who was Ronald Reagan?<br>5. Who was George Herbert Walker Bush?<br>6. Who was Pope John Paul II?<br>7. Who was James Brady? | 1. What was Mount St. Helens?<br>2. What was Tehran?<br>3. What was Chernobyl?<br>4. What was Seoul?<br>5. What is the stock market (New York Stock Exchange)?<br>6. What was Tripoli (or Benghazi)? | 1. What was the Chrysler Corporation?<br>2. What is crack?<br>3. What is a hostage?<br>4. What is a stock exchange?<br>5. What was the budget?<br>6. What was fallout? | 1. What was AIDS (Acquired Immune Deficiency Syndrome)?<br>2. What was aerobic?<br>3. What were safety seals?<br>4. What was exercise?<br>5. What was cocaine? |
| 10 | 8. Who was the Ayatollah Khomeini?<br>9. Who was Marshall Tito?<br>10. Who was Lee Iacocca?<br>11. Who was Terry Waite?<br>12. Who was Rock Hudson? | 7. What is the Persian Gulf?<br>8. What was Kuwait?<br>9. What was Libya?<br>10. What was Grenada?<br>11. What was Iran? | 7. What were missiles?<br>8. What was drought?<br>9. What was the Equal Rights Amendment?<br>10. What was acid rain?<br>11. What were illegal drugs? | 6. What is secondhand smoke?<br>7. What was cholesterol?<br>8. What is test-tube (in vitro) fertilization?<br>9. What was the drinking age?<br>10. What was an artificial heart? |
| 15 | 13. Who was Gorbachev?<br>14. Who was Dr. Martin Luther King, Jr.?<br>15. Who was John Lennon?<br>16. Who was Geraldine Ferraro?<br>17. Who was Jesse Jackson?<br>18. Who was Oliver North? | 12. What was the Berlin Wall?<br>13. What was Lebanon?<br>14. What was South Africa?<br>15. What was Canada?<br>16. What was Moscow? | 12. What was the wreckage of the *Titanic*?<br>13. What was tax reform?<br>14. What was the *Exxon Valdez*?<br>15. What was *glasnost*?<br>16. What were the SALT II talks? | 11. What was stress?<br>12. What is burnout?<br>13. What is the ozone layer?<br>14. What were condoms?<br>15. What was lethal injection? |
| 20 | 19. Who was General Colin Powell?<br>20. Who was Ferdinand Marcos?<br>21. Who was General Manuel Noriega?<br>22. What are the elderly?<br>23. Who was Paul Volcker? | 17. What was El Salvador?<br>18. What was Nicaragua?<br>19. What was the Soviet Union?<br>20. What was Reykjavik, Iceland?<br>21. What was Panama? | 17. What was the *Challenger* explosion?<br>18. What was the *Columbia*?<br>19. What was an earthquake?<br>20. What was the Iran-Contra affair?<br>21. What was *USA Today*? | 16. What was dioxin?<br>17. What was Agent Orange?<br>18. What was calcium?<br>19. What was radon? |

# 42 The Twentieth Century's Final Decade—Part 1

| | History-Making People | Featured on the Evening News | Foreign Relations | The World of Science |
|---|---|---|---|---|
| **5** | 1. Who was Saddam Hussein? <br> 2. Who was Bill Clinton? <br> 3. Who was O.J. Simpson? <br> 4. What were Baby Boomers? <br> 5. Who was Ronald Reagan? | 1. What were cigarettes and liquor? <br> 2. What was New York City? <br> 3. What are civil rights? <br> 4. What was the O.J. Simpson trial? <br> 5. What was Oklahoma City, Oklahoma? | 1. What was Kuwait? <br> 2. What was Cuba? (What was Haiti?) <br> 3. What was France? <br> 4. What was Iraq? <br> 5. What was Israel? | 1. What was AIDS? <br> 2. What is Alzheimer's disease? <br> 3. What is World Health Organization (WHO)? <br> 4. What was aspirin? <br> 5. What was the ozone layer? |
| **10** | 6. Who was Oliver North? <br> 7. Who was Hillary Rodham Clinton? <br> 8. Who was Newt Gingrich? <br> 9. Who was Greg Louganis? <br> 10. Who was Cal Ripken, Jr.? | 6. Who was Michael Jordan? <br> 7. What was the crime rate? <br> 8. What is a budget deficit? <br> 9. What was the beating of Rodney King? | 6. What is the United States? <br> 7. What was Saudi Arabia? <br> 8. What were Serbia, Bosnia, and Croatia? <br> 9. What were East and West Germany? <br> 10. What was the West Bank? | 6. What is a hacker? <br> 7. What is DNA? <br> 8. What is a cell phone? <br> 9. What is the v-chip? <br> 10. What is a bit (binary digit)? <br> 11. What is a bug? <br> 12. What are video (electronic) games? |
| **15** | 11. What is a grand jury? <br> 12. Who was Timothy McVeigh? <br> 13. Who was Bill Clinton? <br> 14. Who was Clarence Thomas? | 10. What are HMOs (Health Maintenance Organizations)? <br> 11. What is Afghanistan? <br> 12. What was a hot-air balloon? <br> 13. What were guns? <br> 14. What is the glass ceiling? | 11. What is the North American Free Trade Agreement (NAFTA)? <br> 12. What was Vietnam? <br> 13. What was China? <br> 14. What was Haiti? | 13. What is Atlanta, Georgia? <br> 14. What was Tokyo, Japan? <br> 15. What was Gulf War syndrome? <br> 16. What was France? <br> 17. Who was Dr. Jack Kevorkian? |
| **20** | 15. What was the Brady Bill? <br> 16. What was the CIA? <br> 17. Who was Mike Tyson? <br> 18. Who was Kenneth Starr? <br> 19. Who was Madeleine Albright? | 15. What is "ethnic cleansing"? <br> 16. What is the Federal Reserve? <br> 17. What was Tailhook? <br> 18. What was the Travel Office? <br> 19. What was Ruby Ridge? | 15. What was Haiti? <br> 16. What was Sudan? <br> 17. What were Kenya and Tanzania? <br> 18. What was Saudi Arabia? <br> 19. What was China? | 18. What was Rio de Janeiro? <br> 19. What was Andrew? <br> 20. What are chlorofluorocarbons (CFCs)? <br> 21. What was Hantavirus? |

## 43  The Twentieth Century's Final Decade—Part 2

| | History-Making People | Featured on the Evening News | Foreign Relations | The World of Science |
|---|---|---|---|---|
| **5** | 1. Who was Jimmy Carter?<br><br>2. Who was the Unabomber?<br><br>3. Who was Judge Lance Ito?<br><br>4. Who was Bill Clinton?<br><br>5. Who was President George Herbert Walker Bush? | 1. What was the White House?<br><br>2. What was Japan?<br><br>3. What is a balanced budget?<br><br>4. What was Los Angeles? | 1. What is an accord?<br><br>2. What were chemical weapons?<br><br>3. What was Mexico?<br><br>4. What was the United Nations?<br><br>5. What was the Panama Canal? | 1. What is abortion?<br><br>2. What was AIDS?<br><br>3. What was Dow Corning Corporation?<br><br>4. What was *Jurassic Park*?<br><br>5. What is the Internet?<br><br>6. What are chat rooms? |
| **10** | 6. Who was H. Ross Perot?<br><br>7. Who was Nelson Mandela?<br><br>8. What is a whistle-blower?<br><br>9. Who was Bill Clinton?<br><br>10. Who was David Koresh? | 5. What was the Mississippi River?<br>6. What was Whitewater (Whitewater Development Company)?<br>7. What was Sarajevo?<br>8. What was Bosnia?<br>9. What is downsizing?<br>10. What is affirmative action? | 6. What was Somalia?<br><br>7. What was the U.S.S. *Missouri*?<br><br>8. What was China?<br><br>9. What was Iraq? | 7. What is an application?<br><br>8. What is cyberspace?<br><br>9. What is tofu?<br><br>10. What is the Global Positioning System?<br><br>11. What is El Niño?<br><br>12. What was Denver International Airport? |
| **15** | 11. Who was James Madison?<br><br>12. Who was Janet Reno?<br><br>13. Who was Vincent Foster?<br><br>14. Who was Rodney King? | 11. What was Puerto Rico?<br>12. What was Columbine High School?<br>13. What was the tobacco industry?<br>14. What was the Twenty-seventh Amendment?<br>15. What was Waco, Texas? | 10. What was Japan?<br><br>11. What was Islamic fundamentalism?<br><br>12. What was North Korea? | 13. What is the World Wide Web?<br><br>14. What was the California Desert Protection Bill?<br><br>15. What was the Ebola virus?<br><br>16. What is gene therapy? |
| **20** | 15. Who was Monica Lewinsky?<br><br>16. Who was Alan Greenspan?<br><br>17. Who was Gerry Adams?<br><br>18. Who was Ron Brown? | 16. What are off-year elections?<br><br>17. What is money laundering?<br><br>18. What was the luxury tax?<br><br>19. What is a line-item veto?<br><br>20. What is insider trading? | 13. What is the General Agreement on Tariffs and Trade?<br><br>14. What was global warming? | 17. What is a hospice?<br><br>18. What is La Niña?<br><br>19. What was the human genome project?<br><br>20. What are photoelectric cells?<br><br>21. What was a computer (IBM's Deep Blue)? |

# 44 Into the New Millennium—Part 1

| | People | The Economy | U.S. and World Relations | Science and Technology |
|---|---|---|---|---|
| 5 | 1. What is a curfew?<br><br>2. What is road rage?<br><br>3. Who was Bill Clinton?<br><br>4. What is Alzheimer's disease?<br><br>5. What is ecstasy? | 1. What was the one-dollar coin?<br><br>2. What was California?<br><br>3. What was the Dow Jones Average?<br><br>4. What is the cost of living?<br><br>5. What is poverty?<br><br>6. What is the unemployment rate? | 1. What is kidnapping?<br><br>2. What is spying?<br><br>3. What were slaves?<br><br>4. What was Israel?<br><br>5. What was the United Nations? | 1. What was currency?<br><br>2. What is skin cancer?<br><br>3. What is virtual reality?<br><br>4. What is DNA evidence?<br><br>5. What is dot com?<br><br>6. What is osteoporosis? |
| 10 | 6. Who was Tiger Woods?<br><br>7. What was a chad?<br><br>8. What is a zero tolerance policy?<br><br>9. What are sweatshops? | 7. What is a fiscal year?<br><br>8. What is a bear market?<br><br>9. What is a credit (or debit) card?<br><br>10. What is NASDAQ?<br><br>11. What is a bull market?<br><br>12. What was Alaska? | 6. Who was George W. Bush?<br><br>7. Who were refugees?<br><br>8. What was the World Trade Center?<br><br>9. What was Afghanistan?<br><br>10. What is Africa? | 7. What is DNA?<br><br>8. What is artificial intelligence?<br><br>9. What is a web browser?<br><br>10. What is heart disease?<br><br>11. What is a "firewall"?<br><br>12. What are hybrid cars? |
| 15 | 10. What is bulimia?<br><br>11. Who was John F. Kennedy, Jr.?<br><br>12. Who was Colin Powell?<br><br>13. Who are Hispanics (Latinos)?<br><br>14. Who was Lance Armstrong?<br><br>15. What was 2001? | 13. What is a product recall?<br><br>14. What was Microsoft?<br><br>15. What is foreclosure (or repossession)?<br><br>16. What is telecommunications?<br><br>17. What is the gender gap? | 11. What was Pakistan?<br><br>12. What was anthrax?<br><br>13. What was Jerusalem?<br><br>14. What was Germany?<br><br>15. What was China? | 13. What was foot-and-mouth (hoof-and-mouth) disease?<br><br>14. What is a beta tester?<br><br>15. What is alternative medicine?<br><br>16. What is mad cow disease? |
| 20 | 16. What was the Gates Foundation (Bill and Melinda Gates Foundation)?<br><br>17. What was the Midwest?<br><br>18. What is reality TV?<br><br>19. What is the Americans with Disabilities Act? | 18. What is the U.S. tax code?<br><br>19. What is the marriage penalty?<br><br>20. What was the federal budget?<br><br>21. What was the federal deficit? | 16. What are "coyotes"?<br><br>17. What is bioterrorism?<br><br>18. What were the United States and Great Britain?<br><br>19. What was Reagan National Airport? | 17. What are timekeeping genes?<br><br>18. What was the neutrino?<br><br>19. What was information?<br><br>20. What were femtoseconds? |

**45  Into the New Millennium—Part 2**

| | People | The Economy | U.S. and World Relations | Science and Technology |
|---|---|---|---|---|
| **5** | 1. What are women?<br><br>2. Who was Hillary Clinton?<br><br>3. What was Florida?<br><br>4. What was the census?<br><br>5. What is obesity? | 1. What was a tax rebate?<br><br>2. What is bankruptcy?<br><br>3. What is Social Security?<br><br>4. What is downsizing?<br><br>5. What was hydroelectricity? | 1. What is slave labor?<br><br>2. What was the Pentagon?<br><br>3. What were the twin towers of the World Trade Center?<br><br>4. What were airports? | 1. What is the Internet?<br><br>2. What is a laptop?<br><br>3. What is spam?<br><br>4. What is the World Wide Web?<br><br>5. What is the ozone layer?<br><br>6. What is global warming?<br><br>7. What is a clone? |
| **10** | 6. What is diabetes?<br><br>7. What is a high school diploma (an education)?<br><br>8. Who was Oprah Winfrey?<br><br>9. What is a stalker?<br><br>10. Who was Al Gore? | 6. What is a debit card?<br><br>7. What is the Federal Reserve?<br><br>8. What is a rolling blackout?<br><br>9. What was Bridgestone/ Firestone Inc.?<br><br>10. Who was Alan Greenspan? | 5. What was the IRA?<br><br>6. Who were the Taliban?<br><br>7. What was China?<br><br>8. What was NATO? | 8. What is a gene?<br><br>9. What was *Mir*?<br><br>10. What is recombinant DNA?<br><br>11. What was the International Space Station?<br><br>12. What are Cox-2 inhibitors? |
| **15** | 11. What are chat rooms?<br><br>12. What was marijuana?<br><br>13. What was Mt. Everest?<br><br>14. What are extreme sports?<br><br>15. What are women? | 11. What is telemarketing?<br><br>12. What are payday loans?<br><br>13. What is the grace period?<br><br>14. What is the total tax burden?<br><br>15. What is the income gap? | 9. What was the trade deficit?<br><br>10. What was the WTO (World Trade Organization)?<br><br>11. What was Vietnam?<br><br>12. What was a missile shield?<br><br>13. What was Iraq? | 13. What are NSAIDs?<br><br>14. What are greenhouse gases?<br><br>15. What are genetically engineered plants?<br><br>16. What is encryption?<br><br>17. What was Mars? |
| **20** | 16. What is physician-assisted suicide?<br><br>17. Who was Elián González?<br><br>18. Who was Condoleezza Rice?<br><br>19. Who are telecommuters?<br><br>20. Who is George W. Bush? | 16. What are interest rates?<br><br>17. What are day traders? | 14. Who was Rudolph Giuliani?<br><br>15. What was al-Qaida? | 18. What were pheromones?<br><br>19. What was Eros?<br><br>20. What were atmospheres?<br><br>21. What was moving? |

# WALCH PUBLISHING

# Share Your Bright Ideas

## We want to hear from you!

Your name_____Date_____

School name_____

School address_____

City _____State _____Zip_____Phone number (_____)_____

Grade level(s) taught_____Subject area(s) taught_____

Where did you purchase this publication?_____

In what month do you purchase a majority of your supplements?_____

What moneys were used to purchase this product?

____School supplemental budget       ____Federal/state funding       ____Personal

## Please "grade" this Walch publication in the following areas:

| | | | | |
|---|---|---|---|---|
| Quality of service you received when purchasing | A | B | C | D |
| Ease of use | A | B | C | D |
| Quality of content | A | B | C | D |
| Page layout | A | B | C | D |
| Organization of material | A | B | C | D |
| Suitability for grade level | A | B | C | D |
| Instructional value | A | B | C | D |

COMMENTS:_____

_____

What specific supplemental materials would help you meet your current—or future—instructional needs?

_____

Have you used other Walch publications? If so, which ones?_____

May we use your comments in upcoming communications?       ____Yes       ____No

Please **FAX** this completed form to **888-991-5755,** or mail it to

   **Customer Service, Walch Publishing, P. O. Box 658, Portland, ME 04104-0658**

We will send you a **FREE GIFT** in appreciation of your feedback.  **THANK YOU!**